Anger Management for Stressed Out Parents:

How to Control Your Emotions and Stop Losing Your Sh*t with Your Kids –

Discipline Your Children Without Terrorizing Them by Yelling

Table of Contents

Introduction 5

Chapter 1: What Is Anger? 9

    How Anger Is Expressed 11

    What Causes People to Become Angry? 11

    Is It Possible to Become Ill as a Result of Your Anger? 12

Chapter 2: Why Are You Losing Control with Your Kids? 14

    What Exactly Are Parental Triggers? 15

Chapter 3: Expression of Anger 21

    Types of Anger Expression 22

Chapter 4: Downsides of Getting Angry 30

Chapter 5: The Effects of an Angry Parent on a Kid 34

    Examples of Anger That May Have Been Detrimental to a Child ... 36

    Your Child's Reaction to Your Anger 38

    How Do Parents Control Their Anger? 40

    How Parents Should Start Calming a Stressed Child 40

Chapter 6: How I Stopped Losing Control 43

    Make a Commitment to Retain Control 45

    Be Prepared for Your Child to Push Your Buttons 46

    As a Parent, Understand What You Are and Are Not Culpable For 46

    Don't Get Concerned About the Future 48

Prepare Yourself for Anxiety 48

Make Use of Positive Self-Talk 49

Take a Deep Breath... 50

Envision a Healthy Relationship with Children 51

Chapter 7: Self-Care for Parents 53

Relax and Meditate 54

Spend Time Outside with Nature 54

Listen to Music 55

Participate in a Book Club 56

Take a Walk.. 56

Write in a Gratitude Journal 56

Use All of The Senses 57

Make Time to Be Alone... 57

Make Time for Friends and Family 58

Review the To-Do List... 58

Make Your Bedroom a Retreat... 59

Splurge a Little on Yourself... 59

Give Electronics a Break... 59

Enjoy Everything 60

Practice Mindfulness.. 60

Chapter 8: A Step-by-Step Approach to Stopping Attacks 62

It Is Normal and Reasonable to Become Angry 62

Steps for Parents to Stop Outbursts of Anger 63

To Express Your Emotions, Use an "I" Message 66

Why Do We Get Angry at Our Kids? 69

What Happens When You Yell or Hit Your Child? 70

How Do You Deal with Your Anger? 71

Step-by-Step Methods to Stop Attacks 72

Chapter 9: How to Approach an Angry Child 84

So, What Are You Going to Do? 86

What Type of Temper Tantrum Is It? 88

Assistance with Behavioral Approaches 89

Identifying Explosive Behavior 90

When Behavioral Strategies Are Insufficient 91

Angry Children Need Confident, Calm Parents 92

Chapter 10: Managing Anger with School-Aged Kids 94

What Exactly Is Anger Management for Kids? 95

Ways to Handle School Age Kids' Anger 97

Chapter 11: Managing Anger with Teens 108

An Angry Teen's Mind 109

What to Avoid 110

What to Do Instead 113

- Eight Techniques for Teaching Anger Management to Teens 115
  - Anger Predictions 115
  - Aggression vs. Anger 116
  - Competence in Assertion 116
  - Physical Symptoms of Anger 117
  - Self-Controlled Time-Outs 117
  - Make Time-Out Rules 117
  - Acceptable Coping Strategies 118
  - Problem-Solving Capabilities 118
  - Role Model 119
- Chapter 12: How to Move On From Anger 120
  - Be Emotionally Aware 121
  - Be Optimistic 121
  - Be Open 122
  - Forgive 122
  - Concentrate On the Present 123
- Conclusion 124

Introduction

Many parents become angry – especially with one another. However, be cautious because your anger will have a significant impact on your child's personality characteristics. Your anger influences how you parent. It has an impact on how you communicate with and discipline your children. If you can't agree on family matters, you won't be able to project a cohesive front when it comes to discipline. Anger management for parents, for example, has been described as one of the top priorities for people who deal with children. A strong relationship with a skilled, loving, and supportive parent is the most critical preventive resource for a child to cope with exposure to aggression. While anger is a common emotion, many parents struggle with communicating and coping with their anger constructively. Parents can strengthen their relationships with their children by learning how to cope with anger adequately.

Given the negative effects of anger and aggressive behavior on individuals' mental health, any stressful and disruptive mother-child relationship may have a significant impact on child growth and family well-being. As a result, parents will serve as a model of aggression for their children.

I am the mother of a child. We despise seeing our children make mistakes. And we don't like having to spend time and effort enforcing the consequences. Instead, we scream and get nervous or stressed out.

We have the option of intimidating, negotiating, or pleading. We assume it works, which means that our yelling or agitation will make our children respond the way we want them to. When that doesn't work, we yell or get more nervous, and our screams become the result. That doesn't work, and everyone is aware of it. Nobody is learning or growing as a result of this procedure, so what else can you do?

In this book, I have blended this amazing knowledge with real-life insights to create a user-friendly book. This book is about coming to terms with oneself on a deep level and trying to recover and contain one's anger. Children cannot select their parents. Unfortunately, many people grow up with the life-altering adversities of socially immature, neglectful parents.

In Chapter 1, you will learn about anger, various anger manifestations, the reasons why we become angry, and how we express our anger. The outcome of being angry.

In Chapter 2, you will learn about the reasons and factors on which you lose control with your children and what triggers your anger.

In Chapter 3, you will learn about anger expressions. Anger isn't necessarily positive or bad; it's just a feeling. Emotions are a natural part of being human, serving as in-built guides to alert us to our surroundings and how we can react to them.

In Chapter 4, we will discuss the downsides of getting angry. We lose control of our minds and bodies to a degree while we're angry, and we do things we'll later regret. Words are spoken and decisions are taken in the "heat of the moment," but they are not intended and would not be done if it weren't for anger.

Chapter 5 focuses on the impact of anger on children, since getting angry causes children to become more violent, both verbally and physically. It frightens and instills fear in children. It has been found to have long-term consequences such as anxiety, poor self-esteem, and heightened anger.

In Chapter 6, you will learn how to regain control. As we know, by feeling angry and controlling your anger in constructive and safe ways, you have the opportunity to set a strong example for your children. All parents get angry occasionally, however, if you can't restrain your anger, it can hurt your kids.

In Chapter 7, you will learn about the ways of self-care for parents. What are the self-care tactics for parents and how should we handle time for self-care? A lack of self-care will lead to a downward spiral.

In Chapter 8, you will learn about a step-by-step approach to stopping attacks on kids. What are the ways to stop child abuse?

In Chapter 9, I will describe how to approach an angry child. An angry kid is battling to manage and survive in the only way they know how at the time. There is usually an explanation for a child's anger issues.

In Chapters 10 and 11, I will explain managing anger with school-age kids and teenagers. How to control their anger? What are the reasons they get angry and how should parents handle it?

Chapter 12 is about how to move on as a parent, what the difficulties are, and how children are affected by them. Even if you're only relocating across town, relocation is a significant event for families. You must pack everything, live in disarray, physically relocate yourself and your family to your new location, and then find out where everything is.

This book will help readers recognize and better appreciate stressed-out parent-child relationships, as well as build fresh, safer healing paths. This book offers a valuable opportunity for self-help and is an excellent guide for stressed-out parents who want to transcend their anger and become better parents.

The secret to successful parenting is in your hands, and you are the one who has absolute power. If you make an effort to behave – even though your children misbehave – you will have a better chance of positively influencing any circumstance. Let's be honest: parenting is the most difficult thing you'll ever do – but it can also be the most satisfying. To become the parent you've always wanted to be, you don't have to know all the right solutions at all the right times; you just have to learn to relax. That's all there is to it. You continue to make decisions based on the higher ideals as you learn to work on calming your emotional reactivity (instead of reacting out of your deepest fears).

Chapter 1: What Is Anger?

Anger is a common human feeling that everybody feels. Anger is usually perceived as an uncomfortable sensation that happens when we believe we have been wounded, treated unfairly, opposed in our long-held beliefs, or when we encounter barriers that prevent us from achieving personal objectives.

The perception of anger varies greatly; how much anger happens, how deeply it is felt, as well as how long this lasts, differs from person to person. People also differ in terms of how quickly they get angry (their rage threshold) and how relaxed they are with becoming angry. Most people are always mad, although others are only angry. Certain people are acutely conscious of their anger, whereas others tend to notice it as it happens. According to some psychologists, the average adult is upset only once a day and irritated about three times a day. Some anger management professionals believe that being frustrated 15 times a day is a more acceptable rate. Irrespective of how much we feel it, anger is a natural and inevitable emotion.

Anger has the potential to be both positive and disruptive. Anger or irritation has few negative health or behavioral effects when it is properly handled. Anger, at its heart, is a warning sign that something isn't right with your world. It grabs your attention and encourages you to take steps to correct the error. However, how you handle anger has far-reaching implications for your mental wellbeing. When you show your indignation, it causes you to feel defensive and angry as well. Blood pressure rises and stress hormones are released. Violence can erupt. You could gain a reputation as a reckless 'loose cannon' that no one likes to be around.

Anger that is out of control isolates colleagues, friends, and loved ones. It also has a strong connection to health issues and premature death. Antagonistic, destructive anger not only raises the chance of dying young but also increases the risk of social isolation, which is a significant risk factor for severe illness and death. These are only two of the many reasons that learning to control one's indignation is a smart thing.

How Anger Is Expressed

Anger can be addressed in a variety of ways; different forms of anger have varying effects on individuals and can result in a variety of acts and signs of frustration. Anger manifests itself in both verbal and nonverbal ways.

It can be obvious when someone is upset based on what they say, how they say it, or the sound of their speech. Anger can also be conveyed by body language and other nonverbal signals, such as attempting to become physically taller (and thus more off-putting), staring, frowning, and fist clenching. Many people are very effective at suppressing their rage, making it impossible to detect any physical manifestations. It is, nonetheless, rare for a physical assault to occur without 'warning' signals first appearing.

What Causes People to Become Angry?

Anger may be used instinctively to help defend territories or family members, secure or protect mating rights, protect against loss of food or other belongings, or as a reaction to other potential threats.

Other motives can be very varied, sometimes logical, often irrational. Irrational anger can indicate a problem with anger management or even acknowledging that you are upset.

Is It Possible to Become Ill as a Result of Your Anger?

When we are mad, our bodies produce the hormones adrenaline and cortisol, which are both produced when we are stressed.

Our blood pressure, pulse, temperature, and respiration can rise as a result of these hormone releases, often to potentially harmful levels. This natural chemical reaction, known as the 'fight or flight' reaction, is intended to provide us with an immediate boost of energy and strength. This indicates that the mind and body are preparing for a war or fleeing from threats.

People who become furious, on the other hand, often are unable to properly control their frustration and can become sick, just as unresolved tension may make you ill. Our bodies are not designed to tolerate elevated doses of adrenaline and cortisol for extended periods or daily.

The health issues that may arise as a result of being upset on a daily or long-term basis include:

- Aches and hurts, most often in the back and brain.
- High blood pressure, which can lead to medical complications such as stroke or heart arrest in extreme situations.
- Sleep issues.
- Digestive difficulties.
- Skin problems.

- Lowered pressure threshold.
- Immune system dysfunction.

Anger may also trigger psychiatric issues such as:

- Depression.
- Reduced self-esteem.
- Eating disorders.
- Alcoholism.
- Drug abuse.
- Self-harm.

As a result, it should be obvious that indignation can be harmful to one's well-being.

Chapter 2: Why Are You Losing Control with Your Kids?

Comprehending the parental causes and coping with the underlying feelings will help your problem-solving rather than blowing up on your child.

I hate putting my children to bed. Rather than the idealized golden hour like it was when they were babies, with story time, snuggles, and songs that put them to sleep, it's been a regular saga of running, nagging, moaning, negotiating, screaming, and, at times, weeping. As soon as dinner is over, I begin to feel nervous. After bath time, I'm already expecting the squabbles between my daughters, aged four and six, over which books we'll read, who will sit on my lap, the precise sequence of songs I must sing, and childhood stories I must repeat until they declare my job finished.

Although I recognize that a lot of my parenting problems stem from my inability to be assertive towards my strong-willed children, I also believe that some of their developmentally acceptable antics irritate me even more than they should. Rather than going into problem-solving mode as they compete for my attention and don't listen to me, I feel lost and lose my patience. This pattern isn't working—it makes me feel vulnerable and powerless, and when we revert to intimidation and deprivation, we all feel bad. I'll have to work out how to fix it.

What Exactly Are Parental Triggers?

A stimulus is something you do in the current moment that causes you to recall a memory from the past. We then behave in ways that are inconsistent with the moment.

A cause always brings up an old wound from our youth, such as not feeling noticed or valued. Since the wound is a lie, we tell ourselves, "No one ever listens to me," we are always looking for confirmation that this is the way the world is. When we feel unheard (for example, when we order our child eight times to sit at the table for dinner), the old story is triggered. What happens when you are a kid who does not feel heard? You're furious and irritated.

These old, visceral emotions from the past will change your attitude, make you irritable and resentful, and prevent you from engaging with your child when they allow you to see your child as the enemy and evoke these angry feelings.

Your child might also serve as a reminder of someone in your life with whom you have a tough relationship, such as a mother, father, or sibling. The most popular cause, though, is that the infant reminds you of yourself, namely the aspects of yourself that you dislike.

Meanwhile, to be a successful parent, you don't need to go too far into your background to find out what's worrying you. You must, however, learn to know the causes. There may be little items that are emotionally triggering due to your own childhood experience, or concerns that strike a deeper chord. However, parents can find their child's behavior very upsetting even though it does not directly address these deep problems. Nobody enjoys doing something nice for others and then never receiving a thank you. Certain universal behaviors can make us insane.

Can you find yourself losing your composure more often than you'd like? Here are six of the most popular parenting factors, along with suggestions for dealing with them:

1. Complaining

To be distracted by complaining, you have to be calm, let's face it. It is a major catalyst and it irritates us and we want our children to be happy. Whining and other annoying behaviors, such as not listening, are common when you have a lot on your plate, and they can be very aggravating.

Before attempting to resolve a symptom, the first move is to check in with yourself, understand that you are being stimulated, and demonstrate self-compassion. Take note, for example, if your first impulse is to scream. Say to yourself, "This is just a computer. My brain has been firing in this manner my whole life. It doesn't have to keep shooting like this." You are not genetically programmed to lose your cool and yell; you can select alternative behaviors. The more you do so, the more it becomes a synaptic pathway.

2. Impoliteness

Many of us were mistreated as infants, and when our children disrespect us, the mechanism is triggered. Your three or four-year-old can say, 'No, I'm not going to brush my teeth! You can't make me', since their main duty at that age is to learn how to wield strength. When a parent is triggered by disobedience, they get embroiled in an unneeded power fight. You would go into problem-solving mode if you weren't triggered. You'd think, 'Wow, you despise this so much that you'll never brush your teeth again.' You do need to brush your teeth, though, because if you don't, germs will chew away at them and cause your teeth to fall out. So, we'll have to work this out.

You may also give them the option of brushing their teeth in the bathroom or the kitchen. That's preferable to keeping your child down so you can brush their teeth, as our parents always did. Every time you engage in a power struggle, you make your kid feel more helpless, and they are more likely to demonstrate their power over you in the future by being rude.

3. "I hate you"

When children say, 'I hate you,' their parents become terrified. And still, it is meaningless; they want to show you how upset they are, the kid is aiming for the most volatile, rudest thing they can say to you. Anger is not a feeling; it is a place. When a kid says, "I hate you," they are not dismissing you as an adult. What they mean is, "I'm so angry; I'm scared I'll never be able to sort it out with you." Is that an acceptable response? Say, "You can be as angry with me as you want. I will still love you. And you can't get that cookie (or whatever the kid wants)."

4. Physical discomfort

When children do something physical to you, either to get your attention or by mistake, parents always lose it. "When they're kicking the back of your seat or pulling on your sweater while you're walking, kids can go to considerable lengths to get our attention." Or whether the child flails about when you're trying to put their jacket on to get them in the car seat and they head-butt you in the face. "You have a fully limbic flash response."

And it's okay to be irritated from time to time. The main thing is to patch the relationship later when you've had time to cool down. Healthy challenges and natural bumps, such as someone crying at you because you're mean to them, are a natural part of existence. Your actions have consequences. Those are completely natural human reactions. They have nothing to do with being a bad guy, being tired, being mean, or being traumatized. They're all bad stuff that makes you feel bad.

5. Siblings fighting

Another major cause is when one of the children is hostile or offensive to the other. Especially if one is specifically targeting the other or being irrational; this triggers the mother bear response. If it has anything to do with your early family relationships, where a friend got away with stuff you didn't. Again, it is normal to respond defensively. There is room for both sympathy and defense. We ought to believe that our children are smarter than we thought, so we don't feel bad if we get angry with them.

Limits are used when one child is continually leaning on the other and distracting them, such as when my four-year-old refuses to let my six-year-old have her "turn" on my lap for story time before bed. It is your responsibility to shield the six-year-old and to set boundaries on the four-year-old. It's also a good idea to spend a few minutes with both of them before story time, so they feel close to me and don't fight for my attention.

6. Spills and mishaps

This common occurrence doesn't trouble me at all, but it drives my normally cool-headed husband insane. It's a perfect analogy because we think everyone has the same reactions, but everyone's causes are different. It would be beneficial for my partner to recall a time when he was a kid, and something was poured on him. It was most likely handled as an emergency. Is this a true emergency? No, it does not. Someone leaked everything, and you have to wipe it up.

If your normal reaction is to automatically accuse and condemn, you should practice a different approach. Take a moment to slow your breathing, lower your head, and utter something you've practiced speaking. Something along the lines of, 'It's OK, guys; spills happen, right?' or 'This happens to everyone; we'll pick it up.' If you've done it a few times, it will become pretty automatic. Later in the day, you will discuss with your child how spills can be avoided in the future.

To try to reduce the impact of the causes, I suggest beginning with just one trigger and trying to adjust the hardwired response. Set a goal for a week or two. You're attempting to generate a new series of responses to construct new neural pathways.

Since working on my main trigger, I don't hate bedtime as often as I used to, and I'm not as irritated by their nagging as I used to be. The most crucial thing is to be aware of when you are activated and to use your stop button: Stop, put down your purpose, breathe deeply, and begin again. Every time I correct my response, I weaken the trigger's control. Any catalyst we have will touch on some very serious problems. And those deep problems for any person will be about how we aren't good enough. As a result, our entire life is at stake. But do you have to dig into all of this stuff in your head right now when you're experiencing problems with your child? No. Instead, we must focus on resources to save ourselves from flying off the handle.

Chapter 3: Expression of Anger

Anger isn't necessarily positive or bad, it's just a feeling. Emotions are a natural part of being human, serving as in-built guides to alert us to our surroundings and how we can react to them.

Anger is a positive feeling to experience; everybody has the right to be angry, based on their situation. Feeling angry can be especially important and warranted in these times—threatening circumstances (acute and persistent threats), civil and human rights abuses, health pandemics, impeded freedom of travel, isolation, financial and routine changes – many of us may feel angry as a consequence of resentment, uncertainty, insecurity, or dissatisfaction.

Assertive anger is a potent motivator. Use assertive indignation to combat anxiety, resolve inequality, and accomplish your life goals.

It is how we handle our emotional responses and behaviors that will be the difference between making lasting change and having to cope with the unintended effects of an angry outburst.

The ten most popular forms of anger expression are mentioned below. See if you can recognize the most common ways you choose to respond in frustration, as well as what core values can underpin your perspective on emotions. Clarifying your views about emotions and your rage behavior style – as well as studying simple ways to control the type of speech – is the secret to managing your emotions in a healthy way that allows you to meet your needs despite offending others.

Types of Anger Expression

1. Assertive Anger

Assertive anger is a very positive way to convey one's rage. If this is your kind of rage, you use your indignation or rage as a motivator for constructive change. Rather than resisting conflict, internalizing rage, or having to resort to verbal insults and violent outbursts, you communicate your anger in forms that affect transformation and get you closer to getting your desires and needs fulfilled – all while causing no pain or harm.

Expressing your indignation assertively allows you to get what you want while respecting the interests and boundaries of others.

Management: It's important to remember that feelings, such as indignation, do not immediately lead to hostility or violence; instead, take some time to consider what could be driving you to choose anger when you've felt rage. Distance oneself from the circumstance if necessary and use calming self-talk ("take it easy, keep cool") to maintain control of your feelings, or use a deep breathing method so you are emotionally relaxed enough to assess what is happening and the choices for responding differently.

2. Behavioral Anger

Behavioral anger is a decision to physically respond to feelings of frustration. This type of anger is physical, offensive, or, at the most severe end of the continuum, lethal. Anger is described as behavior to cause injury to somebody else who does not want to be harmed. This may manifest as smashing or throwing objects, as well as physically threatening or assaulting others.

Using behavioral anger to express indignation also has detrimental legal and interpersonal implications, since this extremely erratic and impulsive behavior weakens the capacity to develop trusting and friendly relationships.

Anger is a useful emotion for action and motivation; if something isn't right, getting angry will motivate one to act to change the situation. Anger, on the other hand, is distinct from hostility or brutality. Anger is a normal emotion, while hostility and abuse are preferred overt behaviors that aim to threaten, belittle, and hurt others.

Try heading for a run or walk if you need to physically release your anger.

3. Chronic Anger

Chronic rage manifests as an ongoing and general feeling of indignation towards other individuals, a sweeping sense of dissatisfaction towards such situations, or, more often, anger towards oneself. It is characterized by a persistent feeling of nagging irritation: the chronic presence of this form of indignation may have serious consequences for one's health and well-being.

Spend more time dwelling on the root factors of the frustration as a management tactic. Your outrage may be warranted, but it is unlikely to serve you well if it is chronic and continuing. If you can pinpoint the root of your anger, you may be able to overcome your internal tension by forgiving yourself and others for previous transgressions. Forgiveness is a powerful and rewarding tool that will help to overcome unresolved hurt and anger. Learning how to convey feelings assertively can be extremely beneficial.

4. Judgmental Anger

Judgmental anger is morally outraged – it is normally a response to a perceived wrong or someone else's failing. What also underpins this is a fundamental conviction that you are either better or worse than someone. While judgmental indignation assumes a morally superior position of righteous rage, it can alienate key allies by disregarding their point of view.

Strategy for management: Commit to investigating the light and shadow in various contexts when things are not as clear as they seem on the table. It's a good idea to subtly test your own firmly rooted beliefs by listening to other people's points of view. You can disagree and also gain insight into potential responses and insights into life's problems without dismissing other people's experiences or tarnishing your image by being condescending.

5. Overwhelmed Anger

Anger that is out of balance is referred to as overwhelmed anger. It normally happens when we believe that we have no control over a situation or set of situations, leading to feelings of depression and anger. This form of rage is typical when we take on a lot of pressure or when unusual life events overwhelm our normal ability to deal with stress. Anger is an emotion that is attempting to warn us that we do not feel like we have enough in the tank to deal with the stressors that are piling up in front of us, even though we haven't found the right language to express it yet.

Management strategy: If you are feeling overwhelming frustration, you must get support. Work on communicating to others – family, friends, and professional colleagues – that you are feeling stressed and in need of assistance. Ask for what you can to motivate you, whether it's babysitting, driving a family member to doctor appointments, taking a couple of hours off to get professional help, a relaxing night without a to-do list, or an extension on a job assignment. By removing external sources of tension, you can restore mental and behavioral control.

6. Passive-Aggressive Anger

Passive-aggressive anger is a form of avoidant anger speech. If this is your normal way of expressing indignation, you most certainly avoid all ways of conflict and will dismiss or restrain any feelings of anger or fury you are experiencing. Passive-aggressive frustration can manifest itself verbally as sarcasm, pointed silence, or veiled ridicule, or physically as pathological procrastination at work. People who show their indignation passively can be unaware that their acts are viewed as offensive, and may have serious personal and professional consequences.

Management strategy: Master assertive negotiation skills and use 'What if?' scenarios to explore the fear of conflict. You are more likely to have your concerns addressed in interpersonal relationships if you improve your ability to express your frustrations and confront a variety of fears.

7. **Retaliatory Anger**

Retaliatory anger is typically an instinctual reaction to being threatened or assaulted by another person. It is one of the most prevalent forms of anger and is fueled by a desire for retaliation for a perceived wrong. Vengeful rage may also be conscious and intentional. It also seeks to threaten others by asserting power over a circumstance or consequence, but it can only help to exacerbate tensions.

Management strategy: If the desire for retaliatory frustration is impulsive or deliberate, it is essential to stop and reflect before acting. Would your enraged retaliation strengthen or exacerbate the situation? Retaliation is an option, and cyclical rage rarely fades in a blame game situation. You will escape the unfavorable long-term repercussions of vengeance by deciding to resolve the immediate confrontation.

8. Self-abusive Anger

Self-abusive anger is a form of humiliation-based anger. Since you've been feeling miserable, inadequate, embarrassed, or embarrassed, you could try to overcome those emotions and communicate your anger by negative self-talk, self-harm, drug abuse, or disordered eating. Alternatively, you might find yourself wimping out at others around you to hide feelings of poor self-worth, which would heighten your sense of isolation.

Management strategy: Educate yourself on cognitive reframing strategies and use them to challenge and change any self-defeating, twisted emotions you might be having. Mindfulness therapy will also assist you in centering yourself in the current moment and dealing with any urges to partake in self-harming behaviors.

9. Verbal Anger

While verbal anger is frequently perceived as less violent than behavioral anger, it may be a type of psychological and emotional violence that causes significant harm to the object of one's rage. It is offensive, if not malicious, in the sense there is an incentive to unleash it by inflicting harm on someone who does not wish for it. Verbal violence may take the form of yelling, threats, mockery, sarcasm, intense blame, or critique. If you have verbally abused others, it is natural to feel embarrassed, apologetic, and regretful.

Management strategy: Relieve stress before speaking, even though the words are on the tip of your tongue. As tempting as it is to respond with the first angry thought that immediately springs to mind when you are irritated, the trick to successfully handling this sort of outrage is merely delaying the urge to lash out. With practice, you can overcome the proclivity for verbal aggression and substitute it with assertive anger language

10. Volatile Anger

Volatile anger appears out of nowhere: if it is your form of anger, you are easily irritated by apparent annoyances, both major and minor. You also cool down immediately after expressing the indignation impulsively. Unfortunately, explosive indignation may be very destructive, as those around you can feel compelled to tread carefully for fear of inciting your frustration. Volatile anger affects your ability to establish and sustain long-term relationships because people need consistency and confidence to form positive bonds with you. Volatile rage, if uncontrolled, will inevitably lead to violent outbursts.

Identify the signs and behavioral symptoms that accompany a volatile eruption and utilize calming strategies (such as breathing exercises) to prevent the indignation from worsening.

There are also other expressions of frustration, but these are the ones that most people use when they are angry or irritated. Anger management is an interesting field of study – there is a substantial body of evidence that the realistic techniques listed above, as well as others, are useful methods for communicating anger and other feelings in a healthy manner without causing harm to oneself or others, and for controlling behavior such that it is productive.

Chapter 4: Downsides of Getting Angry

Anger is one of three poisons. It is referred to as a "poison" because it poisons both the brains of others as well as our own. Anger can be lethal in several respects. We can do damage to others when we are attached, but we can still do things to make others happier when we are attached. When we are angry, we rarely do things that make people happy. Although attachment and anger both poison our minds, anger is especially dangerous to others. Although the attachment is not necessarily immediately dangerous, it can be more harmful in the long run.

Anger is really what burns the seeds of virtue or beneficial karma, the value or positive opportunity that we have accrued in the past.

We will create positive incentives, perform good deeds, gain good fortune in our mindstream as a consequence of these acts, and dedicate it. However, if we get angry afterward, the ripening of positive karma is still hampered. If we don't commit it, the rage will wreak havoc. When we dedicate it, the rage can always cause havoc, so it's the contrast between being in a storm with your windows boarded up versus being in a storm without your windows shuttered. Both cases are injurious but to varying degrees.

We devote the constructive potential we have accumulated to safeguarding our virtue and steering it in the right direction. However, this is insufficient. It is important to avoid being enraged afterward. If we become enraged, for example, at a strong karma entity such as the Triple Gem, our teacher, our kin, or the weak and vulnerable, or if we become extremely enraged, the enraged state will seriously impede the ripening of good karma.

As you know, there are some compelling explanations for why some people, especially those in the workforce, tolerate frustration.

Nonetheless, the negative effects of indignation far overshadow the benefits that can be derived from it.

1. It can make you sick

Anger can set off a chain reaction of physiological reactions. And, in extreme cases, it can not only pose an acute crisis, but it can also have long-term effects on the body:

- Cardiac arrest
- Stroke

- High blood pressure
- Mental health issues

Have you ever used the expression "making my blood boil"? Maybe there's a backstory to everything.

2. It can cause heart issues

When we are angry, our cardiovascular system becomes weak. I don't believe we need evidence to reach that conclusion.

But, if you're looking for details, indignation stimulates blood flow to muscles, raises adrenaline levels, raises cortisol, and so on.

Even though heart failure is typically associated with high cholesterol levels and bad behaviors such as smoking, having rage problems does not provide you with a solid foundation to function on.

3. It can inflict agony on others around you

It's bad enough that you have a habit of violently injuring people when you're upset. The most painful aspect, though, is the physical and psychological harm you inflict on families and friends.

It's unpleasant to be around people who are constantly irritated by trivial matters.

Friends and coworkers begin to ignore you because they are too embarrassed in your presence to be themselves. You begin to strain relations that can take a long time to repair.

That is just your circle of friends. Your family is in a tougher situation.

You're left with your wife or husband. And if you carry down your current path, the only way to break ties is by divorce.

But what about your kids? Is your anger fostering an atmosphere in which they will mature into rational adults?

Your family will be in excruciating agony. However, there are few opportunities for intervention, even if you still don't want to live in these circumstances.

4. It can lead to a shorter life expectancy

Anger coping problems have been linked to a shortened lifetime, according to research.

Chapter 5: The Effects of an Angry Parent on a Kid

Children who are abused are more likely to have adverse physical and mental health consequences. If they grow up with this in their household, it will have an effect on their emotional, financial, and practical lives as adults. The path to these negative consequences is incremental, with related patterns manifesting themselves at each point of life.

Children who are abused at home, for example, are more likely to display at-risk activities in school, lowering their odds of academic performance. Many who do not achieve academically will have this potential risk compounded with the others, lowering their likelihood of succeeding in life any further. It should be remembered that a high degree of anger exposure creates an abusive climate.

Furthermore, these same children have a tougher time understanding their feelings than children from families where anger is not prevalent. They may have greater difficulty in self-control, problem-solving abilities, perceptual processing, emotion socialization, attachment, and trauma.

Studies have concluded that parents of neglected children feel and demonstrate elevated degrees of anger, which translates to the child's experience. It is important to remember that in this analysis, the criterion for abuse was established as substantiated complaints of child protection services or a score on a widely used measure that showed abuse.

The kid who lives with anger lives in intense terror. Their bodies recognize that they are in a dangerous situation and respond accordingly. As a result, they respond to this persistent state of anxiety and mature differently than children who are cared for by adults who have good anger management skills.

Observation is the primary method from which children learn. When you consider the adult to be the child's primary trainer, you know that the action they model becomes the blueprint for how the child will act. When they see aggressive behavior from a primary caregiver regularly, the behavior gradually becomes their own. As a result, these children have matured with a decreased capacity to control their emotions.

Examples of Anger That May Have Been Detrimental to a Child

When anger is shown in the family home, it may become a reflex. When habits grow, they can be difficult to break for a variety of reasons, one of which is that parents may be unaware that they are doing so regularly.

You will begin to understand why any of your activities in your home are providing an atmosphere for your child that is not as safe as you would want it to be by thinking deliberately of your actions in your home. Here are some issues to consider:

- **Do you keep adult communications with your spouse private?**

One of the most important ways that parents express their anger in front of their kids is by discussing adult issues. You may believe you are just conversing or debating, but they do not. Humans do not completely comprehend the use of reasoning until the age of 25, when the portion of the brain fully evolves.

This means that your child would have to depend on the part of the brain that handles emotions to comprehend what they are seeing. Remember that by observing them, you are showing them how to act. It is preferable to keep adult communications private.

- **Do your actions convey love and affection for your spouse?**

Learned behavior is absorbed over time as seemingly insignificant behaviors add up to reshape the structure of a relationship. Children learn how to act depending on what they observe in their surroundings. So, whether they have two parents who aren't polite to each other, are short with each other, or are otherwise unpleasant, they will learn not to approach others in the same way.

Moreover, if they grow up in a household where their parents model love, empathy, and cooperation, they are much more likely to cultivate those characteristics as well.

- **Should you take time to consider how you are behaving?**

When things are happening quickly and there is so much going on, it can be difficult to remember how our decisions affect those around us. We all have times when we check in with ourselves and realize there are things we can do better. We don't get around to making such modifications.

That's also disturbing, particularly when it comes to how we model actions for our kids. While life is hurling itself at us at breakneck speed, they are learning how to act from day to day. What is quick to us happens slowly to them over time, and they learn habits from their parents that their parents do not want them to learn.

There are resources available to help measure the degree to which anger is present in the household for parents who want to get a clearer assessment of the level to which they are showing anger in their house.

While you will need to see a psychologist to get this tool administered, it may be well worth your time.

You've already taken a big step toward improving your behavior if you're able to become more mindful of it. After that, you will continue to investigate the causes of your anger and work to improve your behavior.

Your Child's Reaction to Your Anger

A child's actions can vary considerably based on their mood, what they see, and how they perceive it, among other things. Here are a few forms that children have been observed to pick up on their parents' anger:

- **Anger is directed squarely at the child.**

When anger is directed specifically at kids, they do not learn what you want them to. They tend to internalize the emotion and react by shutting down or acting out. They can also learn how to handle people in the same way as a result of this encounter.

If a child makes a mistake, it is the parent's responsibility to teach them how to do better the next time. This can be done in a relaxed and empathetic manner, using both words and deeds.

- **Anger is directed implicitly at the child**

Children should not need to be shouted at or slapped to feel aggression and anger. These negative feelings can appear in a variety of ways. An irate parent can tell their child to go play in their room and stay there or to sit on the couch and watch TV while being quiet. On the surface, none of these two directives seem to have many flaws, but they do. They encourage disconnection. A child would not grow to be peaceful and comfortable in an unconnected household.

- **One parent shows anger toward the other parent**

Keep in mind that children think emotionally. They are interpreting how your vocabulary, sound, and mannerisms make them sound rather than listening to your words. Then they extend the emotion to the other parent, knowing that it would make them feel bad as well.

At first, the child will feel empathy for the parent who is being screamed at, but in the long term, it is showing the child how to handle their loved ones.

- **One parent expresses dissatisfaction with the other.**

Even if their parents aren't openly arguing, children will tell them that something isn't right. Furthermore, the majority of human contact occurs nonverbally. The child forms their view of what is going on in the home based on what they hear and experience.

They internalize these encounters piece by piece over time, constructing context by connecting the dots. If they witness their parents being short with each other, challenging, and trying to be right instead of connecting, they will understand that this is how they can handle others.

How Do Parents Control Their Anger?

When there is peace between the parents, the children feel it, hear it, and benefit from it. The easiest way to establish continuity in the home with children is to start with marriage. Anger is often associated with harsh punishment, which is rarely appropriate.

Anger is often associated with parental tension, and the irritations that parents experience are often shared by the child. Since there is so much content available online now, dealing with topics like this is better than ever. Parents should pursue conventional therapy (which they can do if they are worried about their situation), seek counseling online, read reputable material, and watch reputable videos.

How Parents Should Start Calming a Stressed Child

Parents who have shown more anger against their children than they would have liked still have a chance to change their ways. Every day is a fresh start, and every moment is a new chance. There are steps parents should take to rebalance their family experience. Here are a couple of ideas:

- **Determine how the child is behaving**

For example, if the child has developed a new fear of the dark, this may be a reaction to how they are handled at home. Use this as a cue to devote more time attempting to communicate with them. Allow them to express their fears throughout any of this period. After that, convince them. By providing them with a better sense of confidence, you will help them learn to confront their fears with the knowledge that they will always have you by their side.

- **Take the opportunity to ensure that they witness intentional displays of compassion**

The positive news about learned behavior is that it can be changed and relearned with hard work and commitment. Of course, this is not the optimal path, but it is preferable to the alternative. If a parent attempts, even if it is in the form of minor movements at first, they will be laying the groundwork for improvement.

Allow your child to witness you kissing your partner. Increase the amount of time you spend at the dining table. Make correlations that can lead to behavioral changes and a closer relationship.

- **Establish family traditions that foster closeness**

Habits have a major influence on character. You will change the character of the family by creating traditions in which the whole family will participate. Do things that please you as a couple. Engage in activities that are positive for the mind, body, and spirit as a group. It doesn't have to be difficult.

We ride our bikes together a couple of days a week. Take a trip to the beach together. About dinner time, we want to bring sandwiches and go. When you're together, make an effort to do the small things that prove you care for each other and want to be with each other. This is all that the kids notice more than anything else.

When parents decide to actively focus on their child's environment in their household, they have already taken the first step toward improving the experience. By committing to discovering the solutions and resources that would work best for their families, they are taking everyone involved on a successful course.

Remember that while the days are long, the years are short. Each stage of growth brings with it its own set of challenges and opportunities. Parents who are aware of their child's development are more likely to react productively.

Chapter 6: How I Stopped Losing Control

Why is it so hard to contain our anger when it comes to our kids? There are several explanations for this, but I believe the biggest one is that we encourage ourselves to get angry and lose control. When we respond emotionally to our kids and lose control, we are allowing our kids to dictate how we act instead of the other way around.

Too often, parents respond to their kids without thought. Parents feel they must automatically control their kids, rather than pausing to consider, "Wait, let me first control myself before responding to my child."

The only way to avoid losing control is to learn what triggers you and to know when you start to lose control. This is an important ability for parents to possess. It is, luckily, a talent that parents should master.

So here is the tip: after you've regained hold of yourself, your kids will normally follow suit. Remember that both calm and fear are infectious. It has been shown that a parent's fear about their child greatly contributed to their child's anxiety.

Consider this: if you can't stay still and in check, you're generating the same atmosphere you're attempting to stop.

Here's an illustration: Assume you're training your child to ride a bike. Your child isn't getting it and is whiny and cranky, as well as talking back to you. Your feelings are a mix of frustration, annoyance, anger, and disappointment. You feel obligated to show him how to ride the bicycle, but he refuses to comply.

Instead, you get angry with your child, who is still struggling. Then it gets harder, they can't focus, and they get stressed. He is feeling pressed to do something, and he responds by struggling.

When something happens, rather than snapping and responding, ask yourself, "How can I remain calm so that I can help my child get where he wants to go?"

Apprise yourself that you are not responsible for getting him to ride the bike; rather, you are responsible for being calm and providing instructions. You should then consider the most appropriate approach to assist him in learning.

Finally, once we lose composure and get angry, we establish the loss that we are attempting to prevent.

Undoubtedly, when we lose control and get angry in front of our kids, we are saying, "There are no grown-ups at home." We're saying that we can't control our fear. And when you attempt to handle your child's behavior rather than your fear, you're thinking, "I'm out of control. I need you to improve for me to feel better."

Nobody wants to lose composure and get enraged; we don't do it on purpose. It just seems to happen. There are, fortunately, things you can do to prepare yourself to remain cool. Several strategies are included below to help you contain your anger and remain calm while coping with your child.

Make a Commitment to Retain Control

Commit to attempting to maintain control henceforth. Take note of what irritates you – is it your child rejecting you? Or does backtalk make you insane?

It is not always possible to maintain composure, and no one can keep their temper under control 100 percent of the time. Nonetheless, resolve to remain patient and strive for that objective.

Usually, the first step is to simply commit to not doing something, to not responding at all as feelings of anger against your child emerge.

Allow yourself a pause to do what you have to do to relax. I make my way out of the bed. I sometimes head into the bathroom or bedroom to get away from the situation. Keep in mind there is nothing wrong with disconnecting. You are not required to respond to your child.

Be Prepared for Your Child to Push Your Buttons

When our kids do not do what we want of them, we get irritated. They either do not listen or do not cooperate.

The only solution, in my opinion, is to predict and agree that your child can press your buttons and to not take it so seriously. In a way, your child is doing their job – they are pushing themselves to the max.

Similarly, it is your responsibility to be calm and ensure that your child understands what the boundaries are and that she is kept accountable if she crosses those limits.

As a Parent, Understand What You Are and Are Not Culpable For

Many parents are unsure of what they are and are not accountable for. And when they accept blame for things that relate to their child, they are bound to become disappointed.

Keep track of what is yours and what is your child's. In other words, what should be in your box and what should be in your child's box.

A box has borders, and beyond those boundaries, it has personal space. Your feelings, thoughts, and responsibilities are all contained within your box. Your child's emotions, feelings, and obligations are all included inside their box.

If you've determined whose box is whose, parents should remain in their box and out of their child's box. This does not imply that you do not parent; rather, it implies that you influence but do not monitor your child.

Your child has duties in life that they must fulfill. Those are stored in their box. Those are your child's, not yours.

If you still believe you are accountable for how things work out, you will get in your child's way, which will increase depression and anxiety.

A parent who efficiently stays outside of their child's box will tell them:

"I'm in charge of assisting you in determining how to solve the dilemma. Still, I do not need to fix the problem for you."

If you believe you are responsible for your child's problems, they will not feel obligated to fix them for themselves. You'll get more frustrated and try harder and harder. And the more you attempt, the less your child attempts. It's a waste of time.

Parents do have obligations. When possible, parents should coach their children. And parents should establish family rules and make sure their kids respond to those rules by enforcing them with effective consequences. The child is responsible for the remainder.

Don't Get Concerned About the Future

We also look ahead and wonder if that's how our kids will be for the remainder of their lives. We're not sure if they'll make it in the real world if they won't even do their homework.

The more we worry about their prospects, the more anxious we get. We begin to fear in our minds that we are not doing a good enough job as parents. We are concerned that we do not know what to do to bring them under our influence.

"Thinking mistakes" is a term used by psychologists. Thinking mistakes are feelings that we have in our heads that do not correspond to fact and are typically pessimistic and self-defeating. Each of these reasoning faults is our inherent propensity to predict the worst-case scenario of any given situation. Things rarely go as badly as we feared. Our brains seem to like scaring us.

As a result, sit in your box and concentrate on what you will do right now. The future is up to your child, and no matter how hard you try, you have no power over it. Even if you do try, the fear will skyrocket, making matters harder for all of you.

Prepare Yourself for Anxiety

Take note of what causes the fear and learn to plan for it. You will note that your family's nerves are on edge every day at five o'clock. All have returned home from work or school, are hungry, and are decompressing.

"How am I going to do this when I know my teen is going to yell at me? What do I do if she wants to use the car and I know she thinks I'm intending to say no?"

Prepare yourself for the dispute that you know is on the way.

Say to yourself, "This time, I'm not going to argue with her." Nobody will compel me to do so. I'm not offering her permission to irritate me."

"No matter how hard you want to pull me into a debate, it's not going to happen," you should say.

Allow yourself to be motivated by how you like to see yourself as a parent rather than your personal feelings.

Make Use of Positive Self-Talk

Talk about yourself. Yes, converse with yourself. In your brain, you can tell yourself, "I'm not going to respond to my child's actions. I'm going to take a look back. Let me take a deep breath."

Self-talk can seem to be a gimmick, but it is an effective weapon. For decades, behavioral scientists have learned about the influence of constructive self-talk. You should train the inner voice to deliver calm rather than fear.

Ask yourself, "What has previously aided me?" Consider what has always helped you overcome your fear. What has helped you to cope with something that made you uncomfortable?

Any time you see your feelings rising, say something to yourself. It can range from "Stop," "Breathe," or "Slow down" to "Does it matter?" or "Is it that important?" Experiment with different words and phrases to help you remain in charge.

I have a mental photo ready to help me relax. I remember a lovely spot that still relaxes me. Try to conjure up that mental image for yourself. Visualizing the location ahead of time will improve your desire to go there automatically when you notice yourself getting angry with your child.

Take a Deep Breath

When you find yourself rising, take a deep breath, pause, and think it over. There is a significant distinction between reacting and responding. When you react, you are devoting some thought to what you want to say. When you respond, on the other hand, you are simply operating on autopilot. It's just reactionary.

You want to answer as thoughtfully as possible what your child says or does. Make sure you take a deep breath before responding to your child and the extra time will allow you to think about what you want to say. To prevent a pot from boiling over, simply remove the lid for a few seconds to allow it to breathe.

Envision a Healthy Relationship with Children

Consider the dream bond with your child in five to ten years. "Is how I'm reacting to my child now going to help me get the friendship I want? Is my answer going to assist me in reaching my goal?"

This does not imply that you should give in to your child's demands or accept his or her bad behavior. Instead, it means that you regard your child with the same reverence that you would like her to treat you. It entails speaking to your child in the manner in which you would like your child to speak to you.

Maintain a visual picture of the perfect relationship at all times. Make the image your target. Ask yourself, "Would my angry reaction be worth it?" Will your reaction bring you closer to your target of having a strong relationship with your child?

When your child irritates you, the thought process at the time is critical. The aim is to be as objective as possible regarding our own and our children's actions.

"What is my child doing right now? What are they attempting to accomplish? Are they responding to the tense atmosphere in the house?"

You don't have to persuade them to listen, but you do need to consider what's going on and figure out how you're going to respond to it. Then you will keep on track and not succumb to counter-productive angry urges.

The act of reasoning itself allows one to relax. As parents, we strive to answer the question, "What is it within my power to do to relax?"

The less we have to respond to, the healthier we are. And the longer we learn about it, the better the result will be. That is the crux of our discussion here: responding thoughtfully rather than merely reacting.

The response comes from the term responsibility, someone once said. In that way, handling our anger entails taking full responsibility for what we'd like to respond to rather than reacting instinctively when our buttons are pressed.

And when we can put our logic ahead of our feelings, we can be better parents.

Chapter 7: Self-Care for Parents

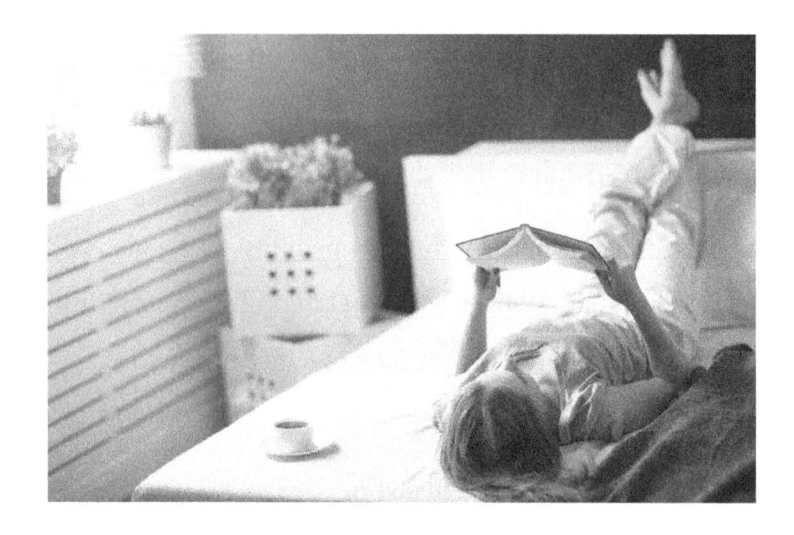

When you become a parent, your attention shifts to taking care of your new bundle of joy. And as your child ages from an infant to a toddler and beyond, you may find it difficult to return your focus to self-care.

A lack of self-care, on the other hand, may lead to a downward spiral. When you don't take care of yourself, you're more likely to feel depressed and exhausted, making it difficult to be a compassionate and patient parent. As a result, you might feel bad or stressed, and self-care could be the last thing that comes to mind.

Taking care of your moral, emotional, psychological, and basic wellbeing will enable you to be the best parent you can be. And if you don't have a spare second to commit to yourself, it's important to schedule some time for self-care. Although there are several self-care solutions for parents, it is critical to play with them to determine the ones that fit well for you.

Relax and Meditate

Maybe just a 5-minute yoga session will make you feel refreshed. If you're new to therapy, psychotherapy might be a nice place to start. There are several applications, forums, and audio and video available to guide you via the methods of meditation.

Several breathing techniques can help you relieve tension in just a few minutes, so you can use them even though you don't have much time. Even if they are brief, a few deep cleansing breaths will do wonders for both the mind and body.

You may also wish to introduce your child to meditation. It's a fantastic life ability that will serve both of you.

Spend Time Outside with Nature

Spending time in nature has been shown in studies to be beneficial to one's psychological well-being. A short stroll through the forest, a stroll on a trail, or time spent tending to a garden will all make you feel refreshed and comfortable.

If you don't have enough chances to go outdoors and enjoy nature, you do have some choices. Looking at landscape pictures can be almost as relaxing as being outside in nature.

Researchers found that patients who stayed in hospital rooms with a window overlooking open fields recovered better than patients who couldn't see outside. Patients that did not have a windshield were then shown landscape photographs. This patient tended to experience less discomfort and fear, meaning that landscape images were beneficial to their physical and emotional well-being.

Green spaces may also be brought indoors with the help of certain indoor plants. Of course, it's not a good idea to buy a bunch of houseplants if the maintenance would add tension to your life.

Book a ride to the beach if you live on the coast. Being by the water also has a calming influence. Research conducted in the journal Health & Place discovered that looking at "blue spaces" decreased a person's risk of mental health problems.

Water has been shown to increase imagination as well as provide a feeling of inner peace.

Listen to Music

If you like to listen to classical music or dance to some 80s songs, music can be a wonderful way to take care of yourself. You don't have to set aside a certain time to listen to music. Switch it on as you're feeding your child or listening to your favorite song while you get ready for the day. It's an easy activity that can go a long way toward improving your attitude and making you feel able to face whatever life throws at you.

Participate in a Book Club

A book club may be used for a variety of reasons. Joining a book club that meets in person will provide you with daily social contact, will encourage you to set aside time to read, and will provide you with something to look forward to each week. Contact the nearest library if you aren't aware of any local book clubs. They can organize book clubs or be able to find one in your area.

Remember that you can still launch your book club. Every week, gather a couple of people to discuss a chapter of a novel. Take turns selecting books and hosting the review at your home or a cafe.

Online book clubs are another choice, but they are not necessarily a suitable replacement for in-person contact. Online spaces can also be vast and impersonal, making it difficult to communicate.

Take a Walk

Exercise can be beneficial to your mind as well as your body. While you do not often have time to go to the gym or partake in an intensive workout, a brisk stroll may be an outstanding self-care technique.

Get your body going for 20 minutes, whether you're pushing a stroller or walking by yourself. A little extra exercise will make you feel more energized for the rest of the day.

Write in a Gratitude Journal

According to studies, people who keep gratitude journals sleep longer and have more quality sleep (something every parent could likely use).

The best news is that keeping a gratitude journal just takes a few minutes of time and costs you nothing.

Make a list of three things you're grateful for before going to bed. Your list could include small items like a sunny day, or it could include major things like being able to pay off a mortgage. In any case, merely reminding yourself of the qualities about which you are thankful will make you feel better about yourself.

Use All of The Senses

When life is hectic, it is difficult to be present. Engaging the senses is a healthy way to unwind and experience inner calm. Light a scented candle, soak in hot steam, listen to calming music, or sip herbal tea. Using one or more of your senses and taking a break from the hustle and bustle can be an easy but powerful way to unwind.

Make Time to Be Alone

Many parents believe that the only place where they can have some alone time is in the restroom. Aside from toilet breaks, it is important to allow yourself a few minutes of alone time.

Even if you just set aside five minutes a day to rest alone, a little solitude will help you unwind. Allow yourself to recharge your battery for some alone time if that means waiting while your child sleeps or until a family member or friend watches your child.

Make Time for Friends and Family

Maintaining social relationships is an essential aspect of self-care. However, finding time to see friends and family can be difficult, particularly if the events do not include the kids.

It gives you anything to look forward to if you plan a potential social outing for yourself (which can be a good self-care strategy in itself). Then, engaging in social interaction would provide an additional boost to your psychological health.

If you plan to go playing golf with a member of the family, have lunch with a neighbor, or have your nails done with your friends, do stuff that will keep you close to other adults.

Review the To-Do List

Tasks do not seem to be effective ways to care for yourself. After all, cleaning and running errands can sound like all you do at times.

Cross anything off your to-do list which has been distracting you, on the other hand, will free up a lot of mental resources. Try to do something on your to-do list that would give you a sense of relief and achievement, whether it's making an appointment for yourself or cleaning that dirty fridge.

You may pick one job to do per day in addition to your regular responsibilities. You will discover that getting stuff done, instead of making them pile up, lets you keep a sense of peace.

Make Your Bedroom a Retreat

When you walk into your bedroom and see stacks of clothes or mess, you can feel more stressed. Making your room into a retreat that you look forward more to entering is a healthy way to take care of yourself. Declutter your bedroom, buy some cozy sheets, and redecorate a bit. A comfortable chair in which to read a decent book or a redecorated closet can make you feel more at ease.

Putting some effort into making your space a sanctuary now would mean that you have a relaxing place to relax at the end of the day.

Splurge a Little on Yourself

It can be tempting to waste money on your kids though ignoring yourself a little. However, it is important to demonstrate to your kids that you respect yourself as well. Allow yourself to spend some time and money on yourself.

Simply purchasing new clothes or spending on a haircut will help you feel better. You may put aside a small amount of money in your budget per month to spend on yourself, or you may just do something good for yourself once in a while. In any case, it is appropriate to indulge yourself from time to time.

Give Electronics a Break

Scrolling via media platforms, browsing the web, and binge-watching TV can seem to be enjoyable ways to unwind. On the contrary, these tasks will often add to the burden rather than alleviate it.

Digital devices will put a lot of pressure on you to still be "on." If you feel obligated to respond to a work email late in the night or you respond to social media posts right before bed, your digital activities could be doing more harm than you know.

Surprisingly, studies suggest that people who nap without a phone in their rooms are happier and more rested. These short tips may be something you'll have to feel more at ease and comfortable.

Enjoy Everything

If you're still in a hurry, there's a fair chance you never get to savor something. Committing to savoring everything is a daily habit. Practice living in the moment, whether you want to savor your first cup of coffee or you want to savor those times when you're snuggling with your child.

Practice Mindfulness

Mindfulness exercises, or even a normal mindfulness exercise, will help you become more present—which is essential for truly savoring what is happening right now. Rather than replaying everything that happened yesterday in your head or worrying about what could happen later today, savoring the moment would allow you to enjoy what is right next to you now.

Don't overlook the most fundamental aspects of self-care: eat a balanced diet, get seven or eight hours of sleep every night, and exercise daily. When it comes to keeping your house clean, don't expect perfection, but please keep up with the essentials, cleaning, and washing.

Then, incorporate self-care tactics into the daily schedule. Bear in mind that the moments when you believe you don't have time to look for yourself are most definitely the times that you need it the most.

Consult the doctor if you are feeling a lot of anxiety and stress, or if you believe you might be depressed. Consultation with a mental health counselor can be beneficial to you. Your doctor, on the other hand, may also want to rule out any physical health issues first.

Chapter 8: A Step-by-Step Approach to Stopping Attacks

It Is Normal and Reasonable to Become Angry

One of the reasons behind this phrase is because your kids understand how to get under your skin. Although, or perhaps because of, the unfathomable depths of your love for them, you may be unready for the strength of your anger. It is natural to be at your wit's end, even though it is distressing and frequently shocking. Anger may build up when you are a parent 24/7, year after year.

No one cares more about your kids than you do, which means the stakes are tremendous, as are the feelings. Everybody has situations when they completely lose it. You may, however, lessen the frequency with which you "lose it" by understanding further about anger and healthy methods to express it. It may take some experience, but you may learn to vent your anger in ways that protect and, in some circumstances, enrich your connection with your children.

Steps for Parents to Stop Outbursts of Anger

As previously said, it is not the anger itself that is detrimental, but rather how it is expressed. You are not required to engage in the fight or flight reaction. There are strategies to cope with your anger in a productive way that maintains everyone's self-esteem. Take note of when you become angry.

The first step is to be conscious of how your body responds when you are angry. Thoughts frequently arrive in your body until you are aware of the matching sensations.

What do you do:

- Do you clench your teeth?
- Do you speak quickly?
- Do you notice your heart racing?
- Do you feel flushed?
- Do you sweat?
- Do you feel hot or cold?

Take notice of where your anger manifests itself in your body. With experience, you will be able to detect the onset of discomfort before it bursts. If you can detect your anger while it is tiny and manageable, you will have a better chance of following the remainder of the instructions without erupting.

This approach, identical to counting to ten, will give you some time to replenish oxygen in your brain and stimulate the reasoning section of your brain, allowing you to do more than just "see red."

You may choose how you want to respond after regaining your control, rather than instinctively responding in predictable, but sometimes unhelpful, ways to the scenario.

Although it is easier than it sounds, you can learn to:

- Slow your breathing
- Relax your jaw
- Talk more carefully and slowly
- Relax your hands
- Take five
- Participate in physical activities
- Visualize a peaceful image, like a rainbow or the sky
- Recite a phrase like "I can manage this," "this too shall pass," or "I can be angry yet still think"
- Consider what is causing you to be angry

You may not be conscious of what is bothering you in the heat of the moment. Getting to the bottom of those underlying sentiments and the causes for them can make all the difference.

If you realize that one of your unmet wants is driving the problem, you may attempt to find ways to obtain what you want, such as a break or time with a friend.

If your children's conduct is the problem, you may study typical child growth to see whether your expectations of them are reasonable. Much of a parent's anger stems from the belief that their children are purposefully attempting to "drive them insane."

You may be able to let go of your anger and react with less aggravation and more compassion if you learn to take the conduct less personally. You are also more likely to appear with more efficient and inventive methods to modify the encounter.

For example, if you know that a normal 9-year-old is hyperactive, you may recognize that forcing the child to sit through a lengthy family dinner is tough for them. After around 30 minutes, they usually pick a battle with their younger sibling. Rather than condemning them and causing a conflict at the table, you might recognize that this is a normal part of being nine and prepare for them to get up and refill water bottles or clean the table.

As you reflect on your event, consider if the term "angry" accurately describes your feelings. Is there an underlying emotion that has to be addressed to better characterize your reaction?

The clearer you are about your feelings, the better you will be able to discuss them and solve difficulties. It might also assist to visualize your feelings on a scale.

Again, the more accurately you can explain your experience, the simpler it will be to moderate your responses.

To Express Your Emotions, Use an "I" Message

Once you've determined what irritates you, you may express your unhappiness with an "I" message. An "I" message's purpose is to express your experience without criticizing or humiliating others.

You accept responsibility for your behavior, which prevents you from having regrets at the end of the day.

The Three Components of an "I" Message:

- I'm feeling... (You should have figured this out in the previous step)
- When I see/hear... (be specific) you call your sister derogatory names
- Because... It is vital to me that you and your partner are kind to one another

Ideally, after utilizing an "I" message, you may tell your children what they need to do to fix the problem.

When confronted with their parents' dissatisfaction, many children feel uneasy. By demonstrating how to remedy the issue, you are preserving their self-esteem.

Examples of Powerful "I" Messages

"I am saddened when I hear you call your sister derogatory names because it is vital to me that you and your sister are friendly to one another. You may apologize to her, and we can discuss what else you can say to her when you don't agree with what she does."

"I get enraged when I see your new bicycle left out in the rain since we just purchased it and I do not want it to rust. Go and put your bike in the shed."

Remember to stay focused on the current issue and avoid bringing up previous wrongdoings.

Consider the following:

- Accept anger as a natural, human, and unavoidable emotion.
- Look for underlying problems.
- Direct your anger towards the proper person.
- Examine your child's expectations.
- Concentrate on the essentials.
- Either exit or wait.
- Do not act as if you are not angry when you are.
- Consider how you will convey your emotions.
- Use relaxation methods.
- Keep it brief, to the point, and in the present.
- Avoid using physical force, threats, and words that accuse or blame others.
- Restore pleasant sentiments by using humor.
- Construct a signal system.

- Apologize.
- Set aside time for yourself.

It doesn't help that there are never-ending stresses in life: commitments we're late for, stuff we've overlooked until the last minute, health and financial concerns – the list is endless. Enter our child, who has misplaced their sneakers, suddenly remembers that they need a new notebook for school tomorrow, is harassing their younger brother, or is plain hostile. And then we snap.

If we're honest, we know that in our more serene periods, we could manage any parenting difficulty far better. But, amid our anger, we believe we have a right to be enraged. How can this youngster be so careless, insensitive, ungrateful, or even mean?

But no matter how vexing our child's conduct is, it does not elicit an angry reaction from us. We see our child's conduct ("He struck her again!") and form an opinion ("He's going to be a psychopath!"), which leads to further conclusions ("I've failed as a mother!"). This chain of thinking results in a runaway train of emotions, in this case, anxiety, dismay, and guilt. Those emotions are unbearable for us. We believe that the greatest defense is a good offense, so we freak out at our child in anger. The entire procedure takes about two seconds.

Your kid may be driving you to react, but they are not the cause of your reaction. Any situation that makes you want to strike out has its origins in your childhood. We know because we lose our capacity to think rationally at those times and begin acting like children, throwing our outbursts.

Don't be concerned. That's quite typical. We all enter the parenting partnership wounded in some manner from our childhood experiences, and our kids bring all of those scars to the surface. We might anticipate our kids acting out in ways that might push us over the edge at times. That is why it is our obligation as adults to keep our children away from the edge.

Why Do We Get Angry at Our Kids?

Parents and kids may stimulate each other in ways that no one else can. Even as adults, we are frequently unreasonable in our interactions with our parents. (Who has more power to irritate you and cause you to act juvenile than your parents?)

Likewise, our children irritate us precisely because they are our children. Psychologists refer to this phenomenon as "ghosts in the nursery," which means that our children elicit profound sensations from our childhoods, and we frequently respond by unknowingly re-enacting the past that is inscribed like lost hieroglyphics deep within our psyches. Childhood anxieties and wrath are extremely potent and may overpower us also as adults. It might be quite difficult to put these spirits to rest.

It's useful to be aware of all of this if we're trying to manage anger. Equally essential, while it motivates us to exercise self-control, we must be aware that parental anger may be damaging to young children.

What Happens When You Yell or Hit Your Child?

Consider your spouse or wife losing their cool and yelling at you. Envision them three times your size, towering above you. Consider that you are fully reliant on that person for your food, housing, safety, and protection. Consider them your principal source of affection, self-confidence, and knowledge about the world, to which you have no other recourse. Take whatever sensations you've evoked and multiply them by a factor of 1000. That is similar to what occurs inside your child once you are angry with them.

Of course, we all become angry at our children, even infuriated at times. The key is to summon our maturity so that we can manage how we express our anger and so reduce its detrimental influence.

Anger is frightening enough. Name-calling or other forms of verbal abuse in which the parent talks disrespectfully to the child have a greater personal impact since the child is reliant on the parent for their fundamental sense of self. And children who are subjected to violence, including slapping, have been shown to have long-term detrimental consequences that affect every aspect of their adult lives, from lower IQ to stormier relationships to a higher probability of drug misuse.

If your young child does not appear to be terrified of your anger, it is because he or she has witnessed too much of it and has evolved defenses against it and you. The sad effect is a child who is less inclined to desire to please you and is more susceptible to peer group pressures. That indicates that you'll have to undertake some repair work. Whether they express it or not, the more we become angry, the more defensive they will be, and so less likely to express it. Our anger is scary to our children.

How Do You Deal with Your Anger?

Because you are human, you will occasionally find yourself in flight or fight mode, and your child will begin to resemble the enemy. When we're swept up in anger, we're physiologically prepared to fight. Hormones and neurotransmitters are coursing through our systems. They make your muscles tighten, your pulse accelerate, and your respiration becomes more rapid. It's tough to remain cool during those times, but we all know that slamming our kids, though providing immediate comfort, isn't what we're doing.

The most essential thing to keep in mind about anger is to not act on it. You will feel compelled to act, to teach your child a lesson. That's your anger speaking. It considers this to be an emergency. But it nearly never is. You can teach your child later if that is the lesson you wish to teach. Your child is not leaving. You are aware of their residence.

So, resolve today to refrain from beating, swearing, calling your child names, or administering any punishment when angry. What about yelling? Never yell at your children; that's a temper tantrum. If you need to shout, go into your car with the windows rolled up and shout where no one can hear you, and avoid using words since they will make you upset. Simply scream.

Your children feel angry, too, so finding constructive methods to cope with your anger is a double gift to them: you not only don't injure them, but you also provide them with a role model. Your child will undoubtedly witness you become angry at times, and how you manage those circumstances teaches children a lot.

Will you educate your child that force equals justice? Do parents, too, have temper tantrums? Is that how grownups deal with conflict? If this is the case, they will adopt these habits as a badge of maturity. Or will you teach your child that anger is a natural part of being human and that learning to control anger appropriately is part of maturing? This is how it is done.

Step-by-Step Methods to Stop Attacks

1. Set Boundaries BEFORE You Become Angry

When we become angry with our children, it is often because we have not set a boundary, and something is grinding on us. When you start becoming angry, it's an indication that you need to do something. Meddle is a good way to avoid aggravating conduct from occurring again.

If your frustration is coming from you for example, if you've had a difficult day and their natural enthusiasm is wearing on you, it might help to explain this to your children and encourage them to be kind and keep the behavior that's bothering you in control, at least for the time being.

If your children are doing something that is becoming increasingly irritating, such as playing games where someone is likely to be harmed, stalling when you ask them to do something, or bickering while you're on the phone, you may need to halt what you're doing, clarify your expectation, and divert them to avoid the situation, and your anger, from growing.

2. Take a Deep Breath BEFORE You Act

When you're this enraged, you need a strategy to de-escalate. Stop, drop (your agenda, for just a minute), and breathe will always help you harness your self-control and transform your physiology. Your pause button is that deep breath. It provides you with an option. Do you truly want to be controlled by your emotions?

Reassure yourself that this is not an emergency. Shake your hands to release the tension. Take another ten deep breaths.

You might attempt to find a method to chuckle, which relieves stress and changes your attitude. Even pushing yourself to grin sends a signal to your nervous system that there is no urgency and begins to relax you. Hum, whenever you need to make a noise. You may try putting on some music and dancing to help you physically release your anger.

If you can set out 20 minutes a day for mindfulness practice, you may strengthen your brain capacity, making it simpler to calm yourself in stressful situations. However, even daily life with children should provide plenty of opportunity for practice, and every time you resist acting out of anger, you rewire your brain to have better self-control.

Certain people still trust the age-old suggestion to pummel a pillow, although it's better if you can do so in secret because witnessing you smash that pillow might be rather frightening for your child. He is well aware that the pillow is a substitute for his head, and that the picture of crazy striking mama will be burnt into his brain. I believe this is a risky technique because research suggests that striking anything – anything – reinforces to your body that you are in an emergency and should remain in flight or fight. So, it may tire you out, however, it doesn't address the sentiments that are fueling your rage and may even make you angrier.

Rather, if you can breathe deeply and accept the angry sensations, you will likely realize that immediately behind the anger are fear, regret, and sadness. Allow yourself to feel those emotions, and the anger will go.

3. Take Five

Recognize that being angry is a horrible starting point for intervening in any circumstance. Instead, take a break and return when you're able to remain calm. Move physically away from your child so that you are not tempted to reach out and forcefully touch him. Simply state, as gently as possible, "I am too angry right now to talk about this. I'm going to take a break and relax."

Exiting does not provide your child a chance to win. It instills in them the gravity of the offense and serves as an example of self-control. Use this time to relax, not to whip yourself up into a frenzy about how correct you are.

If your child is old enough, you may walk into the bathroom, splash some water on your face, and perform some breathing exercises. However, if your child is old enough to feel neglected when you leave, he or she will follow you.

If you can't leave your kids without exacerbating their agitation, head to the kitchen and wash your hands under the water. Then, sit on the sofa beside your child for a few minutes, taking deep breaths and repeating a calming mantra, such as one of these:

- It's not an emergency.
- Children are required to love the most when they deserve it the least.
- My child is behaving out because they want my aid in dealing with their deep emotions.
- Today is all about love.

It is OK to repeat your slogan aloud. It's a terrific example for your kids to watch you handle big emotions correctly. Don't be shocked if your child adopts your chant and begins to use it when they are angry.

4. Instead of Acting on Your Anger, Listen to It

Anger, like other emotions, is as natural as our limbs and legs. What we choose to do with it is our responsibility. Anger frequently teaches us great lessons, but acting when angry is rarely helpful, save in rare cases needing self-defense, since we make decisions that we would never make in a reasonable state. The productive method to deal with anger is to restrict its expression and, once calmed down, to utilize it as a diagnostic tool: What is so wrong in our lives that we are engaged, and what do we need to do to rectify the situation?

Sometimes the remedy is obvious: we need to impose rules before things get out of control, or start to put the kids to bed half an hour earlier or focus on our connection with our child so she stops treating us harshly. Sometimes we're astonished to discover that our anger is directed at our spouse, who isn't fully engaged in parenting, or even at our boss. And sometimes the reason is that we have unresolved anger that spills over onto our kids, and we need to seek treatment through therapy or a parents' support group.

5. Keep in Mind That "Expressing" Your Anger to Someone Else Might Strengthen and Exacerbate It

Despite the prevalent belief that we must "vent" our anger for it not to consume us, there is nothing beneficial in expressing anger "against" another person. According to research, expressing our anger when we are angry makes us much angrier. This, in turn, causes the other person to feel hurt and terrified, causing them to become even angrier. Not unexpectedly, instead of resolving anything, this increases the relational schism.

Furthermore, expressing anger isn't entirely real. Because you are so disturbed within, your anger is directed towards the other person. True sincerity would be sharing the hurt or fear that is causing the anger like you would with a spouse. However, your duty with your child is to regulate your own emotions, not to project them onto your child, so you must be more measured.

The remedy is always to first calm yourself. Then, before deciding what to say or do, understand what the core "message" of the anger is.

6. Wait Before Resorting to Discipline

Make it a priority to never behave irrationally. Nothing says you have to declare edicts on the spur of the moment. Just say something like:

"I can't believe you hit your brother after we discussed how much hitting hurts. I'll think about it, and we'll speak about it this afternoon. I want you to be on your best behavior till then."

Take a 10-minute break to calm down. Don't repeat the scenario in your head; doing so will just make you angrier. Instead, employ the tactics outlined above to help you relax. However, if you've taken a ten-minute break and still don't feel calm enough to communicate productively, don't be afraid to postpone the discussion:

"I'd like to reflect on what just transpired, and we'll speak about it later. Meanwhile, I need to cook dinner and you need to do your homework."

Sit down with your child after supper and, if necessary, impose strong limitations. However, you will be better equipped to listen to his side of the story and respond with fair, enforceable, and courteous boundaries on his conduct.

7. Never, Ever Use Physical Force

85 percent of teenagers report their parents have smacked or spanked them. Despite this, research after research has shown that spanking and other forms of physical punishment have a long-term harmful influence on children's development. The American Academy of Pediatrics strongly advises against it.

Honestly, I am curious to know if the epidemic of stress and anxiety within adults in our society is being exacerbated in part by the fact that so many of us grew up with grownups who harmed us. Many parents downplay the physical abuse they endured because the emotional toll is too severe to bear. Repressing our childhood sorrow, on the other hand, makes us more prone to strike our children.

Spanking may temporarily relieve your fury, but it is harmful to your child and eventually undermines everything beneficial you do as a parent. Physical abuse, and even slapping, tend to escalate. There is also some indication that spanking is addicting for the parent since it allows you to release your frustration and feel better. There are, however, alternative ways for you to feel better that do not harm your child.

Do everything it takes to keep yourself under control, even leaving the room. If you can't control yourself and resort to physical action, apologize to your child, explain to him that striking is never acceptable, and get treatment for yourself.

8. Avoid Potential Risks

Threats made when angry are usually irrational. Threats are only efficient if you are ready to carry them out, therefore they weaken your authority and reduce the likelihood that your kids will obey the rules the next time. Instead, inform your child that you must consider an acceptable reaction to this rule violation. The tension will be much worse than hearing a series of threats you know you won't follow through on.

9. Be Cautious of Your Intonation and Word Choice

According to research, the more calmly we talk, the calmer we feel, as well as the more calmly people respond to us. Likewise, using curse words or other positively contentious language irritates us and our audience, and the situation worsens. We can soothe or disturb ourselves and the person we are communicating with by our tone of voice and word choice. (Remember, you're the example.)

10. Are You Still Angry?

Don't become enamored with your anger. Allow it to leave once you've listened to it and made the necessary modifications. If that doesn't work, keep in mind that anger is always a defense. It protects us from feeling exposed.

Look at the hurt or fear that lies under the anger to get rid of it. Perhaps your son's outbursts frighten you, or your girl is so preoccupied with her pals that she dismisses the family, which saddens you. Your anger will fade once you embrace those underlying feelings and allow yourself to feel them. And you'll be able to intervene more effectively with your child to overcome what appeared to be an insurmountable situation.

11. Focus on Creating a List of Appropriate Techniques to Deal with Anger

When things are quiet in your home, talk to your kids about appropriate methods to deal with anger. Would it ever be ok to strike someone? Is it ok to toss things? Is it ok to yell? Remember that because you are a great parent, the rules relating to your child apply to you as well.

Then, write a list of appropriate methods to deal with anger and place it on your fridge door where everyone in the family can see it daily. Allow your kids to watch you checking it as you become enraged.

- Express your desires to the other person without assaulting them.
- Put on some music and dance your angst away.
- Clap your hands around in your own body and hold yourself when you want to hit.

12. Pick Your Fights

Every unfavorable encounter you have with your child depletes your relationship capital. Concentrate on what is important, such as how your child respects other people. In the grand scheme of things, his jacket on the floor may drive you insane, but it isn't worth bankrupting your relationship. Remember that the stronger and closer your bond with your child, the further inclined he is to follow in your footsteps.

13. Recognize That You Are the Problem

If you're willing to work on yourself emotionally, your child will always show you where you'll have to improve. If you aren't, it's difficult to be a tranquil parent since everything will provoke you to act out. Every encounter we have with our child has the potential to either soothe or worsen the situation. Your child's actions may irritate you, but you are not a helpless victim.

Take charge of managing your feelings first. Your child may not become a little angel overnight, but you'll be surprised at how less angry they act if you learn to remain cool in the face of their rage.

14. Continue to Search for Effective Methods of Correction That Encourage Better Conduct

There are much more efficient ways to punish than using anger, and research shows that using anger to reprimand sets up a loop that perpetuates misbehaving.

Some parents are astonished to learn that there are households in which children are never disciplined, even with repercussions or timeouts, and where parental screaming is rare. Limits are set, and there are behavioral expectations, but they are reinforced through the parent-child bond and by assisting children with the needs and concerns that drive their "bad" conduct. According to the research, these families have children that take more responsibility for their actions at a younger age and are emotionally well-adjusted.

15. Seek Counselling If You Constantly Battle with Your Anger.

There is no shame in seeking assistance. The humiliation comes from failing to fulfill your parental responsibilities by physically or psychologically harming your child.

Chapter 9: How to Approach an Angry Child

What is your first reaction when your child or adolescent is having a tantrum or a full-fledged rage? Do you grow angry and shout, do you stiffen and say nothing, or do you get terrified and give in? Perhaps your response is, "All of the above, depends on the day!" You will not be alone. Dealing with youthful anger and violent outbursts is among the most difficult challenges we face as parents. It is not only difficult to achieve properly, but it is also taxing and may easily leave you feeling discouraged, even if you do not lose your cool. We all know that the aforementioned behaviors aren't beneficial, but why is that? Simply said, if you freeze and do nothing, lose control and shout, or give in to your child's requests, they will realize he can press your buttons – and that it works. Even if your child cannot express it verbally, they realize that if they can terrify you or wear you out by throwing a temper tantrum, they will get their way.

When your child understands that you have specific flaws, they will continue to utilize them since they now have a useful tool to address their difficulties. Instead of facing repercussions or being made responsible, they've devised a technique to get away with it.

You'll be one step ahead if you can recall that something else impacted your youngster initially, whether that was regret, unhappiness, or irritation. Another important concept to grasp is that anger has a function. It alerts us to a problem in the same way as burning your finger alerts you to a hot stove. It hits hard and fast, and the response is instant: Your youngster is sad that he can't go to his friend's house, and you've got a battle on your hands.

When a child, even a tiny child, loses control and becomes angry, they might endanger themselves and others, including parents and siblings.

It is not unusual for kids who have difficulty managing their emotions to lose control and vent their rage toward a caregiver, yelling and shouting, hurling harmful objects, or punching and biting. It may be a frightening and stressful experience for both you and your child. After they've exhausted themselves and settled down, children frequently feel sorry for themselves.

So, What Are You Going to Do?

It's important to recognize that conduct is a kind of communication. A worried youngster is so overwhelmed that he is lashing out. He cannot regulate his emotions and express them maturely. He may be unable to communicate, manage his impulses, or solve problems.

This type of explosive conduct is sometimes perceived as manipulative by parents. However, kids who lash out are frequently unable to deal with their frustration or anger in a more efficient way, such as by communicating and finding out how to get what they want.

Nonetheless, how you respond to a child's outburst has an impact on whether he will continue to respond to distress in the same manner or develop better skills to manage feelings so that they don't become overpowering.

Here are some suggestions:

- Maintain your cool. When confronted with a furious youngster, it's easy to lose control and start shouting at them. When you yell, though, you have a lower probability of reaching them. Instead, you'll make them more hostile and belligerent. As difficult as it may be if you can remain calm and in control of your emotions, you may serve as a role model for your child and teach them to do the same.
- Refrain from giving in. Don't encourage them to continue this behavior by agreeing to what they want.

- Recognize and reward proper conduct. When they have calmed down, commend them on their ability to put themselves together. And when they do try to convey their views openly, calmly, or find a compromise on a point of dispute, commend them for their efforts.
- Assist them in honing their problem-solving abilities. When your child is not unhappy, this is the moment to assist them in practice sharing their thoughts and resolving disagreements before they grow into angry outbursts. You might inquire about their feelings and how they believe you may address an issue.
- Time outs and incentive schemes. Time outs for nonviolent misbehavior can be effective with youngsters as young as seven or eight years old. If a youngster is too old for time-outs, you should switch to a positive reinforcement system for acceptable behavior – points or tokens toward something they desire.
- Stay away from triggers. According to Dr. Vasco Lopes, a clinical psychologist, most kids who have regular meltdowns do so at highly predictable times, such as schoolwork, sleep, or when it's time to stop playing with Legos or the Xbox. The trigger is generally being asked to do something they don't want to do or to quit doing something they do want to do. Time reminders ("we're leaving in 10 minutes"), breaking activities down into one-step directions ("first, put on your shoes"), and prepping your kid for circumstances ("please ask to be excused before leaving grandma's table") may all help prevent meltdowns.

What Type of Temper Tantrum Is It?

The magnitude of a tantrum also influences how you react to it. The first guideline of dealing with nonviolent angry outbursts is to overlook them as much as possible, because even negative attention, such as ordering the kid to stop, can be motivating.

Ignoring a child who is being physically abusive, on the other hand, is not encouraged since it might cause harm to others and your child. I recommend placing the child in a comfortable place that does not allow her access to you or any other possible benefits in this situation.

Try putting the child in a time-out chair if he/she is young (typically seven or less). If they refuse to sit on the chair, move them to a backup location where she may cool down alone, away from the rest of the room. Again, for this method to work, there should be no toys or games in the vicinity that may make it lucrative.

Your child must remain quiet in that room for one minute before being permitted to go. Then they should return to a chair for a time out. What this accomplishes is to give your kid an instant and consistent penalty for their violence while also removing all access to reinforcing elements in their environment.

If you have an older kid who is acting aggressively and you are unable to get her to a safe location to calm down, I recommend distancing yourself from her presence. This keeps you secure by ensuring that she does not receive any attention or encouragement from you. In severe cases, calling 911 may be required to safeguard your and your child's safety.

Assistance with Behavioral Approaches

If your child is constantly lashing out, frightening you, and disturbing your family, you must get professional treatment. There are effective behavioral therapies that can assist you and your kid in overcoming the hostility, relieving stress, and improving your connection. You may acquire strategies for better successfully regulating his conduct, and he can learn to rein in disruptive conduct and have a lot more good connection with you.

- Interaction treatment between parents and their children. PCIT has been demonstrated to be extremely beneficial for children aged two to seven. A therapist advises parents through an earbud while the parent and kid work through a series of exercises together. You learn how to pay closer attention to your child's positive conduct, disregard small misbehaviors, and consistently punish bad and aggressive conduct while keeping calm.
- Parental Management Education. PMT teaches skills similar to PCIT, although the therapist generally works with parents rather than the kid.
- Proactive and collaborative solutions. CPS is a program that is founded on the notion that explosive or disruptive conduct is the

consequence of lagging abilities rather than, for instance, an effort to get notice or test limits. The goal is to educate children on the abilities they need for them to respond to a situation in a more efficient way than having a tantrum.

Identifying Explosive Behavior

Outbursts and mishaps are especially worrying when they occur more frequently, more strongly, or after the age at which they are normally expected from the terrible twos through preschool. Aggression in a youngster becomes increasingly hazardous to both you and the kid as the youngster grows older. And it might cause him a lot of problems at school and with his buddies.

If your child tends to lash out, it might be due to an underlying issue that needs to be addressed. Among the various causes of aggressive conduct are:

- ADHD: Kids with ADHD become quickly frustrated, especially when they are expected to finish schoolwork or go to bed.
- Anxiety: A nervous youngster may keep his anxieties hidden, only to lash out when responsibilities at school or home place too much strain on him. A youngster who "keeps it together" in school frequently loses it with one or both parents.

- Undiagnosed learning disability: If your child acts out at school or at homework time, it might be because the task is too difficult for him.
- Sensory issues: Some youngsters struggle to process the information they get via their senses. Too much noise, people, and even "scratchy" garments might cause them to feel uneasy, uncomfortable, or overwhelmed. This might result in behavior that leaves you perplexed, including hostility.
- Autism: Children on all levels of the spectrum are frequently prone to significant meltdowns when frustrated or confronted with unexpected changes. They frequently have sensory difficulties that cause them to be nervous and irritated.

Given the numerous potential reasons for emotional outbursts and violence, a correct diagnosis is critical to receiving the necessary treatment. You might start with your pediatrician. She can rule out medical issues and send you to a specialist if necessary. A qualified, professional child psychologist or psychiatrist can assist in determining whether or not there are any underlying difficulties.

When Behavioral Strategies Are Insufficient

Professionals believe that the younger a kid can be treated, the better. But what about older children and even younger children who are so harmful to themselves and others that behavioral approaches alone are insufficient to keep them and others safe?

- Prescription medication. Medication for underlying disorders such as ADHD and anxiety may increase your child's reachability and teachability. Antipsychotic drugs such as Risperdal or Abilify are frequently used to treat kids with severe behavioral issues. However, these drugs should be used in conjunction with behavioral methods.
- Retains. Parent training may involve learning how to utilize safe grips on your child to keep both him and yourself safe.
- Household settings. Children that exhibit extreme behaviors may need to spend time in a residential treatment center or, in rare cases, a hospital environment. They are given behavioral and, most likely, pharmacological therapy there. Therapeutic boarding schools offer regularity and organization 24 hours a day, seven days a week. The idea is for the youngster to absorb self-control so that he may return home and behave more appropriately with you and the rest of the world.
- Outpatient care. A youngster with severe behavioral difficulties lives at home but attends a school with a tight behavioral plan under day therapy. Such schools should have trained personnel on standby to manage crises safely.

Angry Children Need Confident, Calm Parents

It might be difficult for parents to learn to handle an angry child using behavioral tactics, but for many kids, it may make a significant impact.

Parents who are self-assured, calm, and consistent can help their children develop the skills they need to manage their behavior.

This may need more patience and willingness to try new tactics than you would with a preschooler, but the result is a stronger connection and a happier house, so the work is well worth it.

Chapter 10: Managing Anger with School-Aged Kids

If you're a parent, you've almost certainly dealt with an angry child. We frequently find ourselves in yelling bouts with our kids, or we tense up, unsure what to do if an angry reaction arises. Anger is a typical feeling in both kids and adults. However, how we articulate and cope with our anger is the way to live in relative calm and feeling at our wits' end. The way to control angry children and adolescents is a lifelong process and a vital skill to master. Toddlers consider their wants and aspirations to be urgent. "I'm going to die if you don't bring me that chocolate or that new dump truck on the shelf." A tantrum is a child's way of protesting having her wants to be denied and experiencing a sense of "powerlessness."

While seeing your toddler spasm in agony over a lost playground session may feel out of the ordinary, anger is a completely normal emotion. Furthermore, it follows youngsters through all phases of growth until they reach maturity. Some of us may have seen more sparks of anger as a result of kids feeling shut away during the epidemic, but parents would be dealing with the developmental challenges of a physical outburst of anger anyhow. It is our responsibility to educate youngsters on the best methods to deal with it.

When a child battles with anger, it is difficult for both parents and kids. Some youngsters become quickly frustrated. They get worked up over seemingly insignificant things. They scream. They may even turn hostile.

If your toddler has anger problems, especially if their anger affects their interactions and life quality, you must give them the skills they need to manage emotions healthily. A mental health professional's advice can also be highly beneficial.

What Exactly Is Anger Management for Kids?

Anger is a warning emotion. It is typically used to respond to danger, but it is also a form of self-expression and, in some cases, a child's means of proclaiming independence. Many factors can incite a child's anger, which can occasionally lead to aggressiveness. In the example of Marie and her elder brother, each youngster launched an attack. Marie got terrified as a result of her reaction and sentiments. Chewing, arguing, and angry outbursts were, as is often the case, waiting around the corner. When children reach school age, their anger typically does not burst into hostility since they have learned to control such impulsive desires. Parents might expect increasingly subtle manifestations of aggressiveness when their children enter school age, such as pouting, sulking, and complaining.

Young children, it turns out, have a lot to be angry about. They're little. They are not permitted to do what they desire. Most of the activities they attempt fail. Elders tell them what is what, and because they are also stronger, they may force them to do it. Three to five-year-olds feel danger even when none exists, or they act irrationally to it. They try to protect themselves by going on the attack. At this point, emotions are difficult to control, and the capacity to pause, listen to the other side, and seek commonality for reconciliation is barely visible.

Adults may find it clear, but a young kid must learn that anger is the term she may give to specific emotional and bodily sensations associated with anger, such as a racing heartbeat, breathing heavily, and a feeling of being overheated. In the heat of the moment, you may assist your kid by noticing and labeling the emotion: "I know you're probably angry right now." She also needs your assistance in identifying the factors that cause these emotions, such as another kid seizing a toy or threatening to damage her; an adult obstructing her exciting plans or appearing to punish unfairly; or her failure to meet a new goal she has set. She'll realize, with your aid, that these are the sort of circumstances that make her want to yell and strike.

Ways to Handle School Age Kids' Anger

Don't raise your voice or become angry at your child during an emotional outburst

Parents frequently respond to their kids' angry outbursts by confronting them and screaming back. However, this will just exacerbate your sense of being out of control. In a crisis, the greatest thing you can do is be cool.

If you are in a vehicle accident and the other motorist is upset at you, if you can remain cool, they will likely start to relax and be rational. However, if you respond aggressively, saying, "What are you talking about, it was your fault," the tension will remain elevated.

So, if your youngster is angry, don't question him. That only adds fuel to the flames. Instead, be patient and wait for him to settle down.

1. Let Your Child Express Their Anger

When your toddler has an emotional outburst, tell him or her, "I see you're angry." If you know why they are angry, you may explain: "I can tell you're angry because you really enjoy swinging on the swing, and we also have to leave the park." Recognize their anger. "It's OK to feel angry," tell them. You want your child to be comfortable with themselves and their feelings. You don't want them to feel compelled to hide their feelings.

2. Avoid Attempting to Reason with Your Child While Having an Angry Outburst

Whenever their kids are angry, many parents I speak with resort to reasoning. And besides, as adults, we employ logic to diffuse heated situations. However, arguing with an angry child is always difficult since they do not have the same ability as we have to pause and reason.

So, while interacting with your angry toddler, you must leave that linguistic space where you feel most at ease and employ a variety of tactics. "Why are you furious at me?" he asks. "You were the one who left your assignment at school," will only aggravate your youngster. Instead, wait till he gets comfortable and then discuss it later.

3. Be Aware of Your Reactions

It's critical to keep an eye on your reactions, both physical and emotional. Your instincts will warn you, "Wait a minute, I'm in the presence of someone agitated." Because your adrenaline is heightened, your heart will begin to beat quicker. Even if it is tough, the secret is to act against it in some manner while being calm.

Remember that you are providing your strength to your children during these difficult times. You are teaching kids how to deal with anger by remaining cool. By being cool, you are not pushing your youngster to a power battle.

Focusing on your reactions can also help your youngster focus on himself since he won't have to worry about you or your feelings. If you do not answer gently, your child will intensify his tantrum to attract your attention. So, to deal with the outburst swiftly and successfully, you'll need to draw on some excellent parenting abilities.

4. Don't Get Physical with Your Child

I received a call from a parent whose teenage kid yelled at his mother and was shoved by the father. The altercation became more heated.

Following that, the son refused to speak to his father because he believed his father owed him an apology. The father, on the other hand, believed that his kid was to blame for the situation and was concerned that apologizing would undermine his authority. Here's what I suggested he say:

"I lost control, and I was wrong to shove you. I sincerely apologize."

That is all there is to it. Nothing else. That's the end of the narrative. We all make errors from time to time, and when we do, we apologize, make repairs, and move on.

Do not discuss your child's part in that event since it is an attempt to blame someone else for your conduct. Instead, you want to educate your child on how to accept responsibility and apologize sincerely.

Don't worry, you'll have more opportunities to work with your youngster on being mouthy or disobedient in the future. However, it is critical to be a good role model and confront your involvement in the fight's demise. Remember that becoming violent with your child, among other things, teaches him to address his issues with aggressiveness.

5. Try a Unique Approach with Toddlers

If your younger child is having an anger outburst, you should step away from him but not entirely isolate him. When tiny kids are unhappy, you should assist them to understand that they can play a role in easing themself down. You might say:

"I hope I can assist you in calming down. Perhaps you can lie down on the sofa for a while."

So, tell them to relax till they feel in control. You're urging them to pay attention to themselves by doing so. So, rather than saying, "You must sit alone for 10 minutes."

"When you start feeling better and are no longer agitated, you are welcome to come out and join us."

You may also provide them with an option. You might say: "Do you have time to organize your things first?" Again, don't question them when they're in that frame of mind.

6. Don't Panic When Your Child Has a Tantrum

When their kids have tantrums or start yelling at them, some parents freeze. The parent is overwhelmed with emotion and either gets immobilized by indecision or succumbs to the child's demands.

If this describes you, you may notice that your child will become angry on purpose to engage you. They'll bait you by throwing a fuss or saying something offensive in the hopes that you'll cave. Don't fall for the ruse. Don't become angry or give in.

In these cases, I believe parents occasionally bargain with their children. Often, parents struggle to manage their own emotions, and as a result, they are unable to adequately train their child at the time.

But keep in mind that if you give in and bargain, even once in a while, you're teaching your child that it's ok to act out. Allow your child to calm down and attempt to coach him to apply his problem-solving abilities later.

When you refuse to negotiate, you are not, in my opinion, being passive. On the contrary, you are intentionally choosing not to engage in a debate. You're saying, "I'm not going to bargain." I'm going to remain calm." On the surface, it may not appear so, yet all of those options are actions.

7. Impose Consequences for Bad Behavior, Not Anger

When your child has a temper tantrum, begins shouting, and loses it, be sure you give him repercussions based on his conduct rather than his feelings.

For instance, if your child curses at you during an angry outburst, punish him afterward for swearing. But if all he does is storm into his room and shout about how unfair life is, I'd let him go. Anger is a normal emotion, and children experience it in the same way that adults do. And they must believe that they have a secure venue to vent their frustrations.

I believe you should allow children to feel angry as long as they are not causing any problems or being rude.

8. Avoid Using Excessively Harsh Punishments

Punishing someone harshly in the heat of the moment is a lost endeavor. This is why. Assume your child is angry. He's throwing a temper tantrum and screaming and yelling at you. You keep repeating, "If you don't get your act together, I'm going to take your phone away for a week. Okay, it's now been two weeks. Keep it up and it'll be a month. Do you wish to continue?"

But, much to your chagrin, your youngster persists, and you continue to escalate the punishment. His anger is out of control, and the more you attempt to punish him to convince him to stop and calm down, the worse he becomes.

That type of discipline is known as: It's known as "consequence stacking." The parent is losing emotional control in this situation. When your child is distressed, I realize how difficult it is to tolerate. It irritates us. But you should attempt to ask yourself, "What do I want my child to learn?"

As well as the answer is almost certainly identified, "I want him to learn not to cry every time he has to do this he doesn't want to do. I want him to understand that when he becomes upset, there is a proper way to deal with it."

This is the worst thing you can do: Get irritated with him and join him. Harsh penalties that appear to be never-ending to your child are ineffective and will just make him angry at the time.

Remember, the idea is to teach your child self-control. Although effective and well-thought-out consequences are important, punitive repercussion piling is not the solution.

9. Take a Break

During coaching sessions, I frequently ask parents about their child's angry outbursts the following question: "When you and your spouse are irritated at each other, what do you do to calm down?" People frequently declare they will take a break and do something on their own for a short period until they can calm down and speak things over.

This strategy also applies to your child, but many parents do not consider it since they believe they ought to have control over their kids. But keep in mind that when someone is angry, you can't argue with them, and you can't rush things.

The basic truth is that if you stay in that anger and continue to engage each other, it will not go away. On the contrary, it continues to grow.

Stop a tantrum from starting by not instantly replying "no" when a youngster asks for something. Instead, take a breather and remark openly, "Let's see how it goes. You're eager to get your hands on that new gadget. Let's get into it." This provides you time to consider the request and, if required, how to decline it or redirect your child's attention. Slowing down and talking about it also helps your youngster grasp the rationale for rejection and accept it more willingly. You want to give your child the impression that you hear him, care about his aspirations, and can be relied on to assist him through life's setbacks.

A location change can sometimes stop rage in its tracks or break a stalemate. You may say, "Let's go to the pet store to see that puppy you like," or "Let's go to the pharmacist and get the hair clips you need."

We'll continue to discuss on the way." Stop interacting with each other right now and return when everyone is less agitated.

10. Encourage Her to Make Use of Words

Wallace shows that children do not automatically know what words to use. You must instruct them on what to say. You can explain to your child: "When you're angry, you need to express yourself," or "I'd want to hear what's bothering you. If you utilize words, I'll understand better and be able to assist you." "When you're angry, say 'I'm angry,' and I'll assist you," you may say. Children internalize your voice and your norms over time. By the age of five, children have developed their superego, which serves as an internal stop sign and aids in the management of violent impulses.

11. Find a Positive Solution

Tantrums were considered as efforts at manipulation for decades. Parents should let their children "cry it out" or risk spoiling them, according to experts. Though parents might indeed slip into the harmful habit of granting every desire of their children to avoid a breakdown, allowing children to cry it out does not teach a kid a more positive approach to conducting herself. In truth, youngsters require assistance in overcoming their anger. It's preferable to let them sink into it.

Try to find a solution: a piece of apple instead of ice cream before dinner or use distractions "I know you're disappointed that it's raining and we won't be able to go to the park. Why don't we go play in the living room tent?" Get your youngster to do something they enjoy. You might perhaps propose an alternative or a compromise.

12. Locate a Quiet Area

If you're out in public, attempt to walk away from the crowd. Concentrate on your child and yourself, not on the opinions of others. This reduces any pressure from spectators and allows you to relate to your child privately. The less noise and commotion there is, the simpler it will be for you to soothe your youngster. "Come sit on my knee and we'll talk things over," you take their hand and offer support.

13. Set a strict limit.

While you want to emphasize that it is ok for your child to be angry, you must also emphasize that physically violent conduct is not acceptable. If your child hurts their sibling, you can tell them, "It's okay to be angry. Your anger is understandable. However, you are not allowed to strike. "We don't strike or kick anyone." You want to steer her toward a good reaction to the event. Describe your limit: "Hitting is painful. Nobody is harmed by us." If the argument seems believable, children are more inclined to cooperate.

14. Demonstrate Appropriate Reactions to Anger

I also advise parents to attempt to be role models for how to cope with anger responsibly. In other words, utilize your anger management as a teaching tool for your kids.

Admitting that you are angry and need time to cool down is not a sign of weakness. It takes a lot of courage to speak these thoughts aloud. Remember, you're teaching your child how to handle his or her anger, and that's precisely what you want him or her to learn.

Kids dislike being angry or having anger problems. They are frequently reacting to dissatisfaction and an inability to handle their own major emotions. Helping your child develop proper responses to anger and other unpleasant emotions will improve their lives at home and school. If you're having trouble, get assistance from your child's doctors or school counselor.

Chapter 11: Managing Anger with Teens

When your teen is angry and yelling at you, many of us are tempted to fight back and yell louder to "win" the battle. But what does that accomplish? When someone presses your buttons or upsets you in any manner, it's normal to want to respond by pushing back or standing up for yourself. This message is frequently inadvertently internalized by us, and it becomes a parent's mantra: "I'm not going to allow my child to walk all over me."

The impulse to shout or fight back is so strong that it might be difficult to resist. However, succumbing to that temptation might be expensive in ways you may not have realized. When you yell or shout at your child, you are merely challenging him and successfully "upping the ante." To put it another way, it raises the stakes of the debate. Not only that, but it prolongs the fight – the more you attempt to "win" and come out on top, the more your child fights back, so you shout louder, and then he begins throwing stuff. When does it come to an end?

Understand that, in addition to extending the disagreement and encouraging your child to continue, shouting back involves giving up power. You and your child are now on the same playing field; you are equal. You are indulging in the same behavior, and as long as you do so, you will continue to receive more of it from your child. By lowering you to his level, your child acquires the impression that he is in control since he can make you lose control by making you angry.

An Angry Teen's Mind

But first, primarily, it is critical to recognize that, though teenagers may participate in adult-like activities or attempt to appear like adults, they do not have adult brains. Adolescent brains are still evolving, and they will continue to do so until they are in their early to mid-twenties. Given this, it is unreasonable to expect children to behave in the same way that adults do. In reality, kids frequently see things in quite different ways than adults, due in part to erroneous or mistaken thinking. The risk arises when individuals utilize their flawed thinking to excuse or excuse their angry actions.

James Lehman describes numerous types of incorrect thinking that children undergo in his Total Transformation Program. Keep in mind that erroneous thinking is not something that someone does on purpose. These are automatic ideas, such as "It's not my fault that I shattered the door. I was furious with my brother." Alternatively, "My instructor is a jerk. Why should I follow her advice?" If you pay attention to your ideas, I'm sure you'll discover that you, too, have flawed thinking from time to time, since it doesn't only happen to children – we all do it.

What to Avoid

Whether you yell, cuss, or call someone a name, there is no excuse for abuse – either by your child or by you. Just as playing the victim role is not a reason for your kid to abuse someone else, your kid abusing you is not an explanation for your shouting, swearing, or name-calling. Being verbally abusive to your child just exacerbates the situation, both in the short term as the fight escalates and in the long term as your child's conduct remains unchanged and your connection becomes strained.

Consequences should not be threatened: It is usually best to avoid frightening your child with particular consequences in the heat of the moment. For example, telling your child, "If you don't stop, I'm removing your computer for three days," is unlikely to cause them to stop shouting and retire to their room. Instead, it will irritate your youngster even more and prolong the conflict. It's more effective to say something like, "If you don't go to your room and calm down, there will be a penalty later," and then walk away.

Attempt to manage your child: This is one of the most difficult obstacles for parents to overcome. Every day, we hear from parents who, without realizing it, are attempting to exert control over their children. I believe this is due, in part, to a widespread misunderstanding about responsibility and what it truly entails. Making your child accountable doesn't result in a child that is always obedient. Even if you constantly give your child penalties when he misbehaves, this does not guarantee that he will always choose to obey the rules. Accountability entails establishing rules and limitations, as well as enforcing consequences when your child violates the rules, period. The idea is not to keep your child from disobeying the rules in the future. You are a limit-setter, not a puppeteer. Allow your youngster to make his or her own decision. Limits and regulations were designed to be exceeded and broken since that is how we learn about repercussions and accountability as humans.

Another way to look at responsibility is as follows: if your child does not comply, somebody will find out, and there will be a "price" to pay, a "cost" for their poor choice in the shape of the potential loss of a luxury that they enjoy. When a youngster encounters this unfavorable event, he may utilize that knowledge to assist him to think about things the next time he considers breaking the rules. In the future, he will learn to question himself, "Is it worth it?" before making decisions.

Get physical: Getting physical typically goes hand in hand with controlling your child. Because your child did not switch off the Xbox when you instructed him to, you try to remove the console or the game controller itself during an argument when everyone's emotions are running high. Or, if your kid threatens to leave the house when she is angry, you try to physically keep her inside by obstructing her route or physically holding her back. To be clear, becoming violent with your child is not a smart choice, first and foremost because it teaches your child that the only way to gain control of a situation is to use physical force. Second, you run the danger of exacerbating the problem. Remember how we discussed the natural desire to fight back? Well, I'm sure you're aware that your teen feels the same way. Many parents have told me about their kids punching back in reaction to the parent becoming aggressive with them first. Don't take any chances. It isn't worth it.

Try to "win": If you're one of those parents who already understands that the best approach to gain control of a dispute with your child is to walk away and cool down, you can skip this tip. Recognize that if you keep trying to "win" every fight with your child, you will lose "the war." To be honest, I dislike using terms like "war" and "fight" because they imply that your child is your adversary. It may feel that way more frequently than not, but remember that your child is not your adversary; he is a youngster who needs to improve his problem-solving abilities.

What I've seen is that most parents I talk to want to raise their children to be respected, accountable individuals who can make it on their own in this world. If this is the case for you, consider the challenges you will face along the path. "Pick your battles, and be prepared to win the ones you pick," advises James Lehman. This implies that before you charge into "war" with your child, ask yourself, "Is it worth it?" It does not imply that you "win" by shouting at your child; rather, it indicates that you succeed by employing effective tactics that will assist you in achieving your long-term goal.

What to Do Instead

Choose your conflicts wisely and consider moving away: As previously said, consider if it is worthwhile to deal with this situation. Is it necessary to deal with it right now? Should you wait till you've calmed down before addressing the issue with your child? Are you having your buttons pressed? Consider the situation carefully and give it some time to calm down. If you still believe the topic is significant after giving it some thought, you may address it later.

Use a business-like tone: In the Total Transformation Program, James Lehman discusses the notion of treating your family like a company. Because you are the CEO of your "family business," remember to address your child in the same tone as a professionally mannered employer would confront an employee with a performance issue. Maintain your cool and stick to the truth.

Self-disclosure: Inform your child that you are experiencing difficulty communicating with them at the moment. It's completely ok to say things like, "It's incredibly difficult for me to listen and talk to you while you're shouting at me," or "When you yell at me, I don't feel like helping you." This is an easy method to establish a boundary with your child and let them know that their behavior isn't working.

Challenge your child's thinking: By "challenge," I don't mean inviting your youngster to continue battling with you by saying things like, "You think you're pretty tough, big guy!?" I'm referring to the fact that his conduct is useless. "I know you want to go to the mall, but talking to me like that isn't going to get you what you want," explain to your youngster. or "I understand you're upset, but yelling at me isn't going to get me to let you play video games before you do your schoolwork."

Last but not least, one of the most effective methods to educate kids is through example. One of the most important aspects of teaching kids how to behave is role modeling. I've said it before, and I'll say it again: don't shout at your child if you don't want him to shout at you. Don't curse if you don't want your youngster to cuss. As James Lehman puts it, "you have to model the conduct you wish to see in your child."

Eight Techniques for Teaching Anger Management to Teens

Teens who can't regulate their anger will have severe difficulties, whether they hurl their cell phone against the wall when an app doesn't work or shout and scream when they don't get their way. Some people may lash out verbally, whereas others become violently hostile. They will struggle in school, relationships, and professions if they do not learn how to handle their anger.

While anger is a common and healthy emotion, it is critical to understand how to manage it. Teens must learn how to manage their anger and express it in a socially acceptable manner. Here are eight ideas and tactics for teaching teenagers anger management skills.

Anger Predictions

Each family has unique ideas on how to deal with anger. Some families have a low tolerance for screaming, although screaming is a common mode of communication in others. Establish ground rules for appropriate conduct and indicate which actions will not be accepted.

Name-calling, physical aggression, or threats are not permitted in your house. Make it clear what the repercussions are for breaching the rules.

Aggression vs. Anger

Teach your teen to distinguish between angry sentiments and aggressive action. Angry sentiments are very normal. Aggressive conduct, on the other hand, is not acceptable. Make it clear that throwing items, slamming doors, or purposefully breaking stuff is never acceptable.

Teens must understand that violent conduct, even if it is merely verbal hostility, can have major consequences. Making threatening comments on social media, for example, might result in legal ramifications. Discuss the intellectual, social, and legal ramifications of aggressive and violent behavior.

Competence in Assertion

Aggressive behavior and anger difficulties can sometimes be traced back to a lack of boldness. Teach teenagers how to properly advocate for themselves.

Discuss the significance of speaking up without infringing on the rights of others. Play through particular scenarios with your teen, like what to do when anyone cuts next to them in line or how to act if they believe someone else is taking advantage of them.

Physical Symptoms of Anger

Teens frequently fail to identify when their anger is rising. They allow themselves to become angry to the point that they can't help but strikeout. Ask your teen, "What does your body feel once you're angry?" Teach children to detect physiological indications of anger, such as a racing heart, clenched hands, or a heated face.

Motivate them to take action if they sense their anger rising. That may entail taking a pause, taking a few calm breaths, or mentally counting to ten.

Self-Controlled Time-Outs

Likewise, instruct teenagers to put themselves in time-out while they are angry. Allow them a little pause to collect their thoughts in a secluded area or persuade them to finish a heated argument with a friend.

Make Time-Out Rules

For example, agree that if anyone from the home becomes too angry to continue a conversation, you will take a 15-minute pause before continuing.

If your teen decides to take a time out, do not pursue them or urge on resuming the talk while they are unhappy. Rather, agree to revisit the topic after a brief cooling-off time.

Acceptable Coping Strategies

Teens must learn how to express their anger in a socially acceptable manner. Teens who lack coping strategies are more prone to become angry verbally or physically.

Assist your teen in identifying coping techniques for dealing with unpleasant feelings such as frustration and disappointment. While painting may help one teen relax, going for a stroll may assist another. Work with your teen to find particular coping methods that aid in the resolution of anger.

Problem-Solving Capabilities

Teens who have poor problem-solving abilities may resort to aggressiveness to meet their requirements. Teach your teen how to solve simple problems.

Encourage them to identify three viable answers if they are dealing with a school project or attempting to address a problem with a friend. Then they may weigh the benefits and drawbacks of each before deciding which one will work best for them.

This might show your teen that there are other methods to handle a problem without resorting to violence. They will get more confidence in their capacity to solve challenges over time.

Role Model

Your actions will educate your teen more about dealing with anger than your words. Expect your teen to manage their anger if you shout, swear, and smash stuff. Set a good example of how to deal with angry sentiments. Show your youngster how to talk about his or her angry feelings and how to express them responsibly. For example, you may say, "I'm angry because you didn't tidy your room like I requested you to. I'm going to go take a few minutes off, and then we'll speak about your punishment."

Chapter 12: How to Move On From Anger

Being a parent elicits a wide variety of psychological emotions, from elation to anguish. Depending on the scenario and the level of support available to you, your sentiments of love, happiness, and pride may swiftly transform into anger, hatred, or guilt. These are entirely natural sentiments.

It is critical to control emotions such as anger and irritation so that you may enjoy parenting and provide a secure, joyful environment for your child. It may be beneficial to speak with other parents; you'll quickly learn that everyone is going through the same emotional and physical rollercoaster.

Coping with issues that have previously angered you and holding those feelings bottled up over time may be a huge load to bear. It may even grow so bad that continually remembering yourself of what irritated you leads to you lashing out against family and friends. It might be so awful that you may do or say things you don't intend. This is what bottled-up anger can do. When an issue, such as a grudge or animosity, is not addressed appropriately, it might threaten your connection with individuals you care about.

You may be asking what you can do to better control and manage your anger in an appropriate and even constructive manner. Below are the ways to handle your anger and move on in life.

Be Emotionally Aware

Emotions may have varying effects on people, and knowing how to move on or accept them may be important character-building skills. Instead of reliving the incident that enraged you and thinking about what you might have done differently to prevent feeling the way you do, accept your feelings now. Anger puts you in a frame of mind where you are aware that something is wrong and that it needs to be handled. When you've decided that this anger will not benefit you, you may make a deliberate effort to comprehend what's going on and begin to let go of what's burdening you.

Be Optimistic

Although being optimistic is easier said than done, reframing circumstances and relationships more positively may have a good impact. Bitterness can influence how you think, behave, and perceive others. Learning to forgive the individual who sparked your angry sentiments and embracing a mood of optimism is extremely doable, and may be made much simpler with expert assistance.

Be Open

One reason why bitterness and anger persist is that individuals keep it locked up. Consider anger to be a corrosive substance in a container. The liquid will corrode the container over time. Anger may do the same to someone who does not let it out in a controlled and appropriate manner. Sitting down with someone, even if it is the person who has irritated you, and discussing your feelings and how a particular incident has harmed you may release a great load off your shoulders. It's also a good idea to do this in a therapy context with someone well-versed in these habits.

Forgive

This may be the most difficult aspect of dealing with your emotions, but to truly move on from your anger, you may need to make a concerted effort to forgive the person who offended you or put you in the situation that caused you to feel the way you do. Remember that we are all flawed human beings. We do and say things we don't always mean, or we make off-the-cuff statements that seem innocent at the moment but may be devastating afterward. Be generous in how you perceive other people's actions toward you and in determining whether to give them the benefit of the doubt or cut them some slack. Don't give another person's actions or words power over you.

Concentrate On the Present

Returning to our previous point, concentrating on the present rather than the past might also assist to relieve your anger. Acknowledging that the past is the past and that you will not be able to change the circumstances that enraged you is a critical step in letting go of your anger. Rather than worrying about what-ifs, concentrate on what you're doing right now. Remember that being forgiving and moving on much exceeds being unforgiving and wallowing in the past.

Conclusion

The book discussed anger problems and parenting stress solutions in families with normally developed children. Everyday strains of parenthood have an impact on the quality of parenting children get, as well as the happiness that parents get from the process of child-rearing.

Parents do so much, and anything challenging a child does can be magnified in terms of the impact. It's a recipe for difficult interactions because everyone's struggling. Your anger is normal, but how you handle it is crucial. Knowing where your anger comes from can help. It's normal to be angry.

Parents' prenatal expectations and experiences, personality, attitude, beliefs, and daily events all contribute to how stressful their children's conduct is for them. There is minimal uncertainty in the stressfulness of actual behavior issues in youngsters. It will be critical to pay attention to the prominence of distinct developmental phases, longitudinal processes, and transitions between periods. Natural developmental changes that children go through at different times generate settings that might exacerbate parental stress. The book discussed anger issues and their remedies in the context of parental stress processes in families with properly growing children.

The accumulated daily stressful experiences of parenting may influence the character of parent-child connections over time. A difficult situation may also give opportunity for constructive growth in parent-child dyads. Many parents can manage effectively with their children's frequently tough or demanding conduct. I conclude by stating that mild stress can be adaptive in the sense that it maintains an ideal level of alertness while also stimulating personal growth.

We prefer to blame it on someone else over something they just did, but that is not true; other people do not make us angry, and until we grasp that, we are frequently locked in a cage of rage for a lifetime. In most circumstances, the source of our suffering is not clear and might be imperceptible to the human eye, causing bleeding in the brain and even death. We need to talk about a new meaning of love.

Let's keep it basic: why do we become angry? The answer is pain, generally a lifetime of it. Think about how irritated you can be just from a minor headache that lasts for a few hours. Pain disrupts our entire emotional well-being. To be healthy and happy, we all need to feel intuitively loved more than anything else. Many of us have never witnessed love like that; instead, we've always had to be responsible, clever, or attractive for others to like us, but that's just trading; it's not true love.

I've spent my entire life being angry with others and blaming them for how I felt. My wrath has just dissipated when I feel appreciated. When I'm loved, I don't have to control or manage my anger; it just goes away.

Even when all else has failed, I witness anger go and be replaced with calm and contentment. You are about to transform the world around you, and you don't have to do it alone, which is both terrible and irritating. I'm not blaming anyone; our ignorance of true love has just been passed down through generations. Happy people simply do not behave improperly, such as when they are upset, for example.

We can assist our children to reach the same results. It will be almost like beginning again in parenting and life, as you will learn how to be a happy person and a true parent, and your kid will acquire life skills that will benefit him or her for the rest of their life.

You won't believe the improvements you'll notice in your child, yourself, and your entire family if you do it regularly. In the words of one parent, "after reading this book, you'll have skills you can apply right away so you may make permanent good changes in your connection with your children beginning right now." This book will show you what it's like to become more unconditionally loving as you let go of your anger.

CPSIA information can be obtained
at www.ICGtesting.com
Printed in the USA
LVHW081940250621
691133LV00002B/116